Sync Async

Making progress easier
in the changing world of work

LYNNE CAZALY

Lynne Cazaly

Copyright 2022 Lynne Cazaly
www.lynnecazaly.com

All rights reserved. No part of this publication may be reproduced, stored in a retrieval system or transmitted in any form or by any means, electronic, mechanical, photocopying, recording or otherwise, without the prior written permission of the copyright owner, except as provided by international copyright law.

National Library of Australia Cataloguing-in-Publication entry:
Author: Lynne Cazaly, 1964 -
Title: Sync Async: Making progress easier in the changing world of work

ISBN: 978-0-6454737-0-4

Subjects: Work.
Leadership.
Productivity.
Change.
Creativity.
Communication.

Cover design, hand drawn font, illustrations and layout by Lynne Cazaly.
Research assistance by Myra May Sabaldan Lahoylahoy

Disclaimer: The material in this publication is of the nature of general comment only, and does not represent professional advice. It is not intended to provide specific guidance for particular circumstances, and it should not be relied on as the basis for any decision to take action or not take action on any matter which it covers. Readers should obtain professional advice where appropriate, before making any such decision. To the maximum extent permitted by law, the author and publisher disclaim all responsibility and liability to any person, arising directly or indirectly from any person taking or not taking action based on the information in this publication.

The Sync Async wording

The pink 'Sync Async' cover design was created on my iPad Pro, using Procreate drawing app and an Apple Pencil. And it is my handwriting.

I tried many different colours, fonts and brush styles over several days and then as I felt it was getting close to the look I wanted, I slept on the idea and then it was a definite 'yes' in the morning... for me anyway!

The intention with the style is to show grouped-together strokes that are imperfect. They are individual and yet together they create the letter. They're not perfectly lined up and they don't start or finish at exactly the same point, but they are mostly aligned.

This is my hope with asynchronous work; that leaders and organisations continue to shift from controlling expectations of perfection, and instead move towards greater trust, flexibility and choice ...that is aligned.

Table of Contents

Introduction	7
Part 1: How did we get here?	**23**
What is sync async	31
Over collaboration	37
Bad meetings are still bad	39
The seven conditions	46
The 3 illusions of synchronous work	64
Part 2: Where do we go from here?	**75**
It's all about progress	80
When to sync async	82
Artefacts of actuality	88
Get out of their way	93
What is your preference?	
Part 3: Skills, Tools and Techniques	**123**
Skills for sync	125
Tools for sync async	150
Techniques for sync async	167
Taking action	178
Where else could you async?	185
Summary	191
References	196
About the Author	198

Lynne Cazaly

Introduction

Lynne Cazaly

Who'd have thought that a virtual musical performance might inspire people to new and different ways of working?

It was a virtual performance of 'What the world needs now is love' by students from Boston Conservatory at Berklee and Berklee College of Music that turned out to be a sweet example of how to make progress when we may not be here and now in the same location.

The student-made performance and video were the brainchild of Shelbie Rassler, a senior composition major at Boston Conservatory.

When music classes were online, she was 'eager to bring her community together.'

Her plan was to rally an entire orchestra to record the song. All they had to do was take a video of themselves singing any part of the song or play an instrument. From real instruments to pots and pans and rice in a saltshaker!

She and her colleague cut all the videos up and arranged them into the beautiful piece you'll find on YouTube (or the link in References)

The feedback to the finished work was overwhelming and it clearly showed how people can work together, collaborate and create beautiful work, even when they aren't in the same location, or even performing at the same time!

It's amazing how it worked out so well. A choir or orchestra still performing as a whole group but not in the same location.

Not only were they not working in a co-located, same studio situation, but they recorded their performance at the times that suited them. The product was still possible. And it was still brilliant. Oh, and it was probably easier, cheaper, quicker and cleverer to do the performance this way.

And a live performance with everyone there at the same time in the same location will still be possible when it is and when warranted. It will still happen. But now we know for sure that we don't all need to be there, now, to make great progress on very good work.

Others followed creating musical performances with orchestras, rock bands, ballet performances, choirs and many other artistic endeavours.

From music to movies, to healthcare, broadcasting, technology, software, education, IT, human resources, learning and development, engineering, governance and financial services: all of these sectors are experiencing changes to the way they have worked for years. And even more changes are possible… and needed.

Despite us thinking that we might be working as well as we can, the thought of pushing for more productivity can be a drag. What if we thought about making progress instead? Let's go then…

Please tick all that apply:

○ **Waiting for busy peoples**

Have you been waiting on someone to get back to you so you could set up a meeting and discuss something?

Perhaps it's about getting started on some work, preparing a quote or proposal or defining a project scope. You can't start without meeting them to understand the situation, get the details, find out what they need, how you can help them and what to start on first.

You might have tried calling them but they're just so busy.

○ **Let's find a time**

Have you struggled to 'find a time'?

Can you do Tuesday at 9am? Ok, good, let's send the invite out.

Nope?

Next day, Aaron, Lisa and Raj will be on leave. Denise has covid and Brigitha has another meeting at that time.

Ok, let's push it out to next Tuesday. No? Thursday then, the afternoon.

Oh, it's school holidays, Easter...

OK, let's look at 10 days' time then. 2pm on the

Thursday? 9am on the Friday. Lunchtime, midday on the Friday, let's squeeze it in between that other meeting and grab a 10-minute lunch break. It's really urgent now, we've got to find a way to bring this whole group together or we'll never be on the same page. We're already losing time, traction and progress.

- **Can I just grab you; it will only take two minutes?**

You're asked for a 'quick chat', and it will only take a couple of minutes. They want to 'grab you' to talk about something… now.

Thinking it will only take a couple of minutes you say 'yes'. You've got some time before your next meeting starts in 20 minutes. It shouldn't take that long, should it?

You start chatting and it turns out that what they want to know is a bit bigger or more complicated than what can be handled in a two-minute quick chat.

Before long, you realise you've been on the quick chat call for 35 minutes and now you're 15 minutes late for that other meeting.

- **No time for work**

You've had a day where you've been in meetings all day, back-to-back. Your team might be trying to consult and collaborate as much as they can to be connected and work well together. But as a result of going to so many team meetings you might find that you are getting drawn into work that isn't your own or being asked for input on tasks that aren't related to your role, but you don't want to let the team down.

You might feel like you're doing well, getting through the day's meetings as they appear in your schedule but at the end of the day feel like you're not making progress on the important pieces of projects and events that are very much part of what you're expected to do.

- **Wrong time zone**

You want to contribute to an event, committee or piece of work but you're disappointed to hear the time zone you live in doesn't work for them. The team or group already covers several global time zones and having someone from yet another time zone is just going to complicate things further.

They tend to believe the whole committee, group or team must meet and work together in the same time zone at the same time.

For your time zone, that would end up being 4 am! They don't want to shift things around and think they're being delayed by having to work with you.

You're disappointed that despite your skills, knowledge and commitment, where you live makes you unsuitable.

○ **Deleted and invisible**

You're working with two colleagues preparing for a major event, like a presentation. Despite them suggesting two or three meeting times, you can't make any of the times for an online call. They go ahead and meet without you, at a time that suited them. You didn't get to contribute, participate or add anything to the conversation beforehand and you didn't hear or learn anything about what they talked about afterwards. Despite this being a group effort, you feel excluded, invisible and left out of the process no matter how hard you've tried.

Did you tick any of these? How many?

What's in common with all these situations?

They all default to **synchronous** work; work in real time, with everyone or most people present. Synchronous or same time work is most often the default in our workplaces today – online or in person.

When we awaken to this default or habit we have of going real time with people for work, we'll see just how much of our effort, energy, time and resources are being stolen from us, as if we have no choice.

But we do have a choice. With a greater awareness of

using less synchronous work and more of the alternate - **asynchronous** work, where we work at a time and in a way that is more flexible and suitable for us - we'll find we're able to make greater progress on all our tasks, projects and goals, with much greater ease.

Over the past 12 years I've been working with teams, leaders and organisations helping them work in new and creative ways.

In this book, I'll share some of the key tools these teams and businesses use to work more productively, creatively and collaboratively – because ultimately, they're more effective, individually and as a team and organisation.

In **Part 1** we'll look at **how we got here**, souped up on sync work. We'll check out the conditions that have created sync work, and the illusions we have about it.

Part 2 will address **where do we go from here** and when, why and how to bring more async work to your everyday.

In **Part 3** we'll review the **skills, tools and techniques**, great sync async-ers use.

We'll wrap with a direction to further thinking, reading and learning to sharpen your sync async game.

A big part of synchronous work is for people who want things now or want to make a resolution now thinking the most productive way of doing that is to get on a call and sort it out. Now. Everything now. "It will only take a minute."

And sure, some things do.

But plenty don't.

Who is this for... and why?

This book is:

For you, in your own practice or business, as a freelancer or a consultant, or in your role in an organization... You are an individual who can exercise their free will to do things in certain ways.

You can immediately begin to change some of the ways that you work, for greater progress, to release pressure and expectation, and free up your schedule.

You will recognize techniques, tools and methods that when combined and put into practice, will help you make getting started on tasks and progressing them easier. Specifically, some of the techniques will help you involve yourself in work that is more relevant for you and untangle yourself from work that is time wasting, irrelevant or of no/low value.

For your team, project, board or committee who find themselves in back-to-back meetings – whether online or in person. It could completely change how your team functions, and in turn, lift morale and boost engagement and enhance the things you are able to achieve.

Yes, it could take a while to get used to working deliberately in these ways, but this could become the greatest path to freedom, flexibility and choice in your working day, week and year. Not to mention your career!

For your business, agency or organization, there is a cultural, philosophical and structural shift that can occur with deliberate and strategic sync async work. As trust grows, engagement lifts, progress is greater, and stress will reduce.

But it will require some of your leaders to think and work in ways that may challenge them. Particularly the control freaks, the ones who micromanage, the ones who want to be 'across everything', the ones who have meetings as their primary work task or who thrive on the power that meetings give them. These are behaviours and styles that need to change, and soon.

People don't leave organizations, they leave leaders. And leaders who are not able to lead a synchronous/asynchronous work team, are the leaders who are falling behind and becoming outdated … and worthy of leaving.

Where are you with new ways of working?

There will always be new and different ways to do things. Some things become better for our personal effectiveness and group wellbeing, other things help us achieve better outcomes or results.

Try looking at it this way:

There is THE WORK and then there is THE WAY WE DO THE WORK. You may be immersed in the work and not conscious of how you can do that work better.

Oh… and there is also the WORK ABOUT THE WORK which doesn't even help us get the work done!

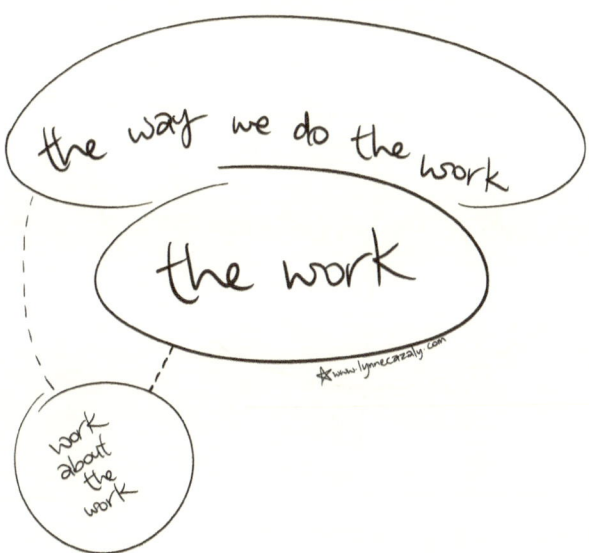

There are already hints of async-ness across our work world. When people put in their email footer that they wrote and/or sent the email at a time that suited them and that you can read it at a time that suits you, they're saying, "I get sync async; you can too".

Just because you received it now doesn't mean you have to respond now.

Sync async is not only about productivity. It's not only about outcomes. Or just about engagement. Or only about contribution. It's all of them. All four. … and probably more.

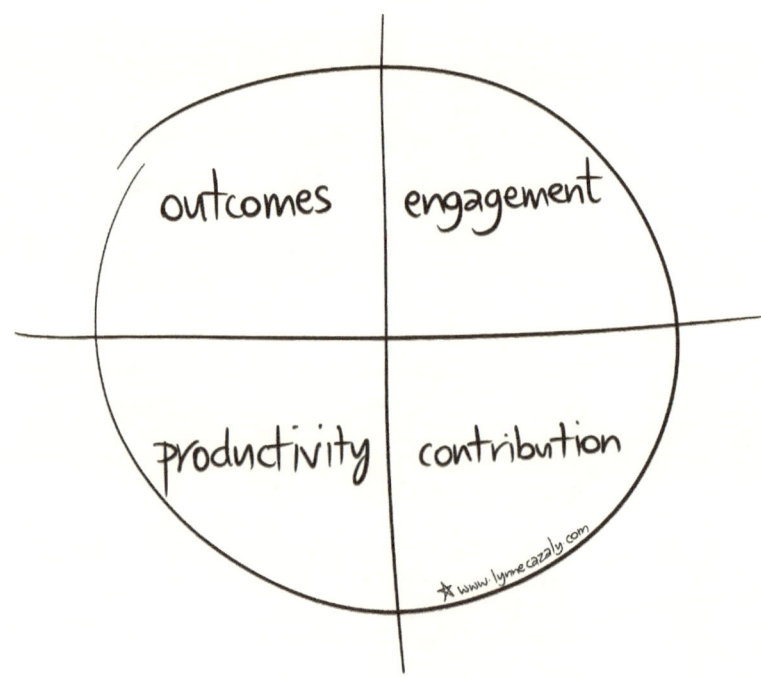

Many workplaces across the world, across industries and sectors are changing the way they work. And it can be new, challenging, confronting even, to re-work how we work.

I like to think of it like this: it's a scale of change, as I shift from having an **old** mindset of **'there is only one way to do this work'**, and that I can shift, bit by bit, towards newer ways of thinking about work. The **new** mindset is: **there have to be other ways to do this work.**

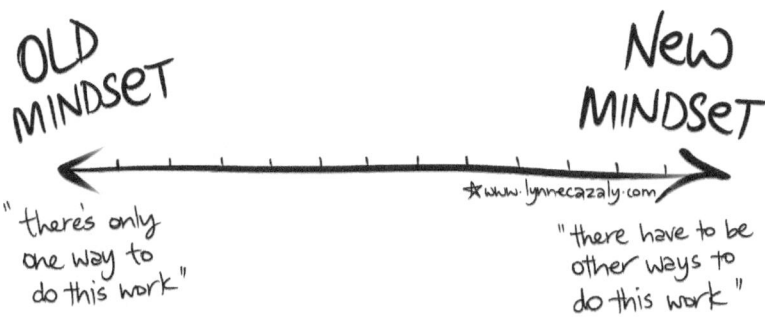

Thinking in new ways can come as a result of frustration or exasperation. If things are difficult, complicated, involving so many people that we don't seem to be getting anywhere, it's a good time to think, 'there has to be another/a better way.'

And there usually is!

Now... sync async work may not be new for you. If so, this next bit IS for you:

If this is 'not new' for you

Oh, hi there. If you think while you're reading this – 'there's nothing new here' - great. You're all good, knowledgeable, and operating with a great sync async balance. Well done you!

But who do you work with, for and in collaboration with? As soon as you get drawn into a sync situation that could have been async, think again.

Your role here is not just to know about this stuff. Or just to do it, only for yourself.

Yours is now a leadership role to help others, to share practices that work. It's time to take on a greater role than just knowing or doing this stuff. It's now about sharing, shaping, extending, encouraging, leading, facilitating, assisting, guiding and supporting.

Take on those roles if this isn't new for you. Because it most certainly is new for someone in your world, and you could be such a great support, resource and ally for and with them.

Do that if it's not new.

PART 1

How did we get here?

Lynne Cazaly

Let's look at how we got to this space where we're questioning how we work and the balance of sync and async ways of doing work.

We'll check out 7 conditions that are impacting this need, why we sync by default and some of the illusions we might have about synchronous work. We'll check out how to shift from passive to active ways of working.

Lynne Cazaly

Life reflected in work

To quickly check the temperature, we look at a thermometer or ask our smart devices. To check what's happening for humans, we use memes. Memes! Memes! Send me memes!

This one from the iland.co clothing company from Instagram.

It happens socially as much as it happens at work. It's

not just you - it's us. All of us. It's life! And it's not really going to change unless we change something about the way we think about meeting up and doing our work... and living.

More memes? Ok, let's check the **way** we work:

> Ways to contact me
> ↓ ranked ↓
>
> 1. Text
> 2. DM
> 3. Email
> .
> .
> .
> 97. Sky Writing
> 98. Smoke Signal
> 99. Call

@melbournemadness

This one from Melbourne Madness Instagram account.

And there it is. Don't call me. Don't speak to me. I'll look at stuff when I'm ready.

Interesting to see phone calls rating so low. That's a synchronous way of communicating – we connect, at the same time. And many of us experience anxiety on the phone so we're happy to let it go through to voicemail and then never listen to the messages anyway!

But psychologists are onto our anxiety about our phone and talking to real humans in real time, warning us that 'it's still not something you can really avoid completely. You can book a restaurant reservation or a doctor's appointment online, but you need to call when you're running late. You can email a job application, but then you have to wait for the special type of hell that is the phone interview.'

Cari Romm in 'Psychologists explain your phone anxiety' suggests the four reasons why we're shifting further away from real time things like phone talk:

- You don't know what the other person is thinking
- You're under time pressure
- You feel like you're being judged, and
- You just don't do it all that often.

To get over it, Romm says psychologists recommend exposure therapy; the more you do it, the less daunting it will be.

Yep, we can send people on telephone training programs or insist that they do it more so that they get used to it. But perhaps we're missing the point here: perhaps we are forcing people into a way of communicating – an old way - that they don't feel comfortable with or is not their preference. If we keep trying to 'make them do it' perhaps the results and outcomes won't be as we hope.

What if we shifted our perspective and let go of that pressure to 'do it like this' and instead generally changed the way we're doing things, allowing people to work in more of the ways that suit them?

I think that's what this sync async thing is all about.

The flexibility people want most isn't remote work. It's to set their own hours.

They want to control their time – when and how much they work.

Offering freedom sounds like a risk, but squashing it is also a risk.

Stars are the first to leave.

- Dr Adam Grant

What is Sync Async

Sync = same time

Sync or synchronous is when we are doing something at the same time. Working on something in each other's presence, online or in person.

Sync work includes things like:

- Meetings: scheduled and unscheduled
- Quick chats and conversations
- Phone calls
- Catch ups
- Sessions or workshops
- Retreats … things like that.

Many companies have forced employees to work on the same schedule. As Kenzo Fong says in 'The future of work is asynchronous', 'if you're getting your work done on time and efficiently, why does it matter when or where it's done?'

So, this leads us to…

Async = different time

Async is when we may still be working together on a project or piece of work, but I do it when it suits me and in ways that might work better for me. And you, you do it when and how it suits you too.

As Fong continues, asynchronous work is 'when work happens for different people on their own time. Consider a worker in London and one in Los Angeles. Based on a 9-5 work culture, they would have only a few hours to collaborate and work together. With an asynchronous work style, work becomes more like a relay race where one could set tasks and deadlines for the other without the expectation to respond right way.'

Async work includes using tools and applications to help like:

- Email
- Task boards
- Text messages
- Chat
- Uninterrupted work time
- Documentation
- Video and audio messages or files
- Shared documents
- Visual collaboration tools
- Direct messages
- Comments and annotations
- Transcripts and subtitles
- … and more.

Musicians create great work, recorded and live, remote

and async. It happens all the time. Many stories abound about how a backing track was sent to a singer and they 'dropped in' their vocals. Separately. Not everyone, and everything you hear is recorded live and in the studio at the one time.

I'm a Steely Dan music fan and the two founders, Walter Becker and Donald Fagen recorded the majority of their hit songs (like, say 'Kid Charlemagne') but would keep working on different sounds for the guitar solo. They'd bring in a range of different session guitarists one after the other to get them to do their take on a solo and then drop the track in to check how it sounded for them. Then they'd choose the one they thought worked best for the song. Larry Carlton, genius guitarist and another of my favourite musicians was the 'winner' on this track. And it's a fine guitar solo!

Movies are produced and made asynchronously too. News bulletins are produced asynchronously. It's like a patchwork of async stuff put together. Not everyone gets together at once, all of them waiting at each location, following each other around all day, waiting for that person to do their bit to camera and then traipsing off to the next location. It sounds ridiculous when we imagine it like that. They'd only end up creating one or two segments of news. And movies would take five times as long and cost 30 times as much!

Instead, when working async on a news bulletin, there could be around 30 items reported on including video footage and audio plus live reporting all put together by people working at different times, in different locations.

So many elements of today's world work together better when they work in asynchronous ways. As a result, this may not seem 'new' to you. But what's new is the deliberate, strategic and flexible approach to working in these ways. Some sync, some async. And how much we can apply it across our work.

As you go along through this experience of sync async, (and I hope you do less sync and more async), you'll find experiences and opportunities that are:

- accidental

- deliberate

- strategic

and

- experimental.

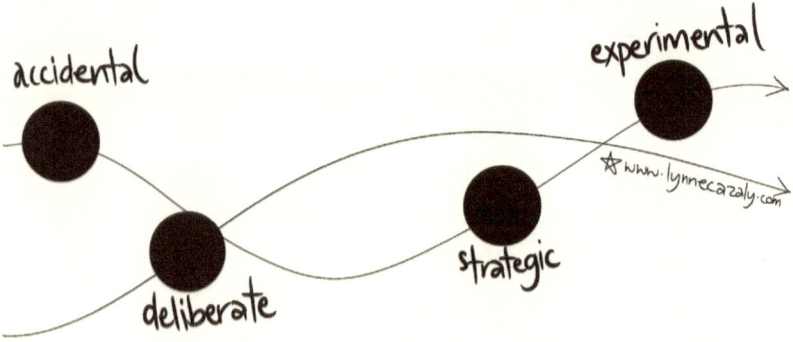

It could be **accidental** that you've done something async and didn't really think about it. Great. Otherwise, just start somewhere with something. See what you need next. Try async at first. Then sync. Then a bit more async. Then some more sync. But to try and do it all sync. Nope.

Allow sync async moments, meetings, work and interactions that are **deliberate**.

Plan ahead more and map out your work with a greater **strategic** view. How might you handle the elements of the project you're about to lead on? Which pieces will you try async instead of sync? Which pieces normally default to sync?

And then allow more **experimental** situations. The push for doing things 'right' and 'perfect' is strong. Try something you usually do sync and see how it goes async.

My sense and experience is that the way we work is all of these things, all of the time. Accidental, deliberate, strategic, experimental.

In person to remote to hybrid to…

To be talking more about sync async ways of working has come about because many people were forced to work remotely from home during the COVID-19 pandemic.

Not everyone, but many people. While many people are opting to stay at home, many are returning and plenty of organisations are crafting their hybrid model: some people will be here, some will be there, some could be anywhere.

So many people have worked longer hours, longer days and work has gobbled up what was their commute time with still more work.

In 'Remote Work Should Be (Mostly) Asynchronous', Steve Glaveski says, 'telling people to log off at 5pm misses the point entirely, because it fails to address the reason for excessive workloads and rising stress – that is, how we work.'

Hmmm, yes, we need to change **how** we work.

Over collaboration

The push to work together and collaborate has been a growing trend particularly over the past decade or so.

People working together, sharing ideas and opinions, generating energy and connection, and creating great work.

But perhaps there is too much and we've begun to 'over collaborate'. Do we collaborate too much, too often in real time leaving little time and space for individual work?

Rob Cross, from Babson College thinks we do and says that 'pre-pandemic, about 85% of people's work was spent on the phone, on email or in meetings.' It's now gone up an extra 5 – 8 hours a week. For many people, this means they're working beyond their 'normal' hours, creating additional and unnecessary workload and leading to stress, illness and longer-term burnout.

Cross says, 'we've moved from scheduling 45–60-minute meetings to trying to cram in a series of 30-minute meetings, which means that you have to be more intense, as well as switch across contexts… you end up with longer to-do lists.' He says, 'people can be 'emailed to death and meetinged to death'.

It's the 'to death' thing that's driving a need for greater change.

I was out at a restaurant earlier this evening and thinking of how chefs and kitchen staff in restaurants may do meal preparation when there are no customers in the restaurant. The chef who prepared the ingredients for the meal you're eating might be home sitting on the couch at the time you actually eat the meal. Not everyone needs to be there all the time to make wonderful things happen.

Bad meetings are still bad

We're also here because of all of those meetings we're in all the time. There's way too many of them and most of them are broken. Still. The meeting culture we've been following for centuries isn't changing swiftly enough to suit our changing requirements for work.

It's not that meetings are bad. Well, yes, they are. Nothing will radically change about meetings. Endless articles suggesting you have a clear agenda and purpose for the meeting still don't change the fact that a meeting brings together people in real time and then sucks up that time with an almost negative return on their investment.

They've been the same boring episode for centuries.

'Meeting procedure' as it was called and born in the 19th Century was based on parliamentary procedure - oh yawn, yes, that's the fundamental problem with them! We've been meeting for millions of years, in caves, out on country and on lands that may not have been our own. Being in conversation with others in person, is not new.

Try as many of us have — me included — meetings aren't really getting better quickly enough. They've not rapidly transformed the way many might have hoped.

As Louise Thomson, leadership made easy expert, said recently: 'I was in two online meetings yesterday – both started late and went overtime. We have before us an opportunity to determine what's important and very important and the courage to make a call on meeting attendance.'

In my book 'Leader as Facilitator: How to inspire, engage and get work done', and the accompanying workshops and training programs, I focus on helping leaders develop better facilitation skills. These are the highly nuanced skills that help you guide a group through a process to an outcome.

Facilitation – from Latin, meaning 'easy' or 'with ease' is about trying to make the leadership, the meeting, the progress easier. And there are some brilliant skills to learn. I still believe this and run this program for in-house clients and as a 1:1 mentoring program for leaders and business owners who want to add this wonderful capability to their consulting skills. A lot of consulting is trying to make things happen for a client, internal or external to the business. If you can apply some of the clever skills of facilitation you can make it easier for you and them. And facilitation can happen in sync or async. It's about making the progress easier.

Still, no amount of training, books, podcasts, posts or systems are ever really changing how we meet; not quickly enough or on a wide enough scale. Sure, your team's meetings might have improved. But still, still, we see, hear and experience broken meetings that:

- waste time

- don't function effectively

- don't achieve outcomes

- lead us to more work, and

- create round and round 'let's have another meeting' confusion.

So, because meetings just ... suck... many leading organisations and teams are enjoying 'meeting free days'. They're experimenting with different days of the week where they simply don't have meetings.

In 'The Surprising Impact of Meeting-Free Days', in MIT Sloan Management Review by Laker, Pereira, Budhwar and Malik, results of a survey of '76 companies with more than 1,000 employees each and operations in more than 50 countries' is presented.

They had all 'introduced from one to five no-meeting days per week (prohibiting even one-on-one meetings) during the past 12 months.'

- '47% of the companies .. reduced meetings by 40% by introducing two no-meeting days per week.
- 35% instituted three no-meeting days, and
- 11% implemented four.
- the remaining 7% eradicated meetings entirely.'

So, what happened? Did they get anything done? Did people miss each other?

The impact they say was profound!

'Autonomy, communication, engagement, and satisfaction all improved, along with a drop in micromanagement and stress, which caused productivity to rise.'

Co-operation went up. People liked using the other tools available to work and communicate. People felt more trusted and valued… and they were more engaged.

Fear not. Ditching some meetings is going to make things better… not worse.

And when you do meet, it takes astute and nuanced facilitation skills to take a synchronous real time meeting and make it work well.

Could we create an environment then, where poor meetings won't survive? They just won't happen because no one would attend! Oh, the shock of it! They'll end up being a meeting of one: the convener or host will be there and the rest of us will be working in a sync async mode. And preferably async.

That's it. Don't meet. Well, less than you currently are. Adopt these meeting free days and email it instead or post it in a shared working document where the work is actually being done. Why are you talking about it real time in a meeting and then going away to create a document and starting work? Start the work now… without the waste of the meeting.

Right now, you may think you have too many emails and too many meetings. Get rid of a heap of the synchronous in real time work and you'll have more time for deep, productive and clever work, contributing to tasks and projects ...primarily asynchronously.

We have spent so much of our working life in a synchronous mode. 'Let's meet to talk about it, to plan it, to get to know each other some more, to nut it out'.

As Steve Glaveski says in 'Remote Work Should Be (Mostly) Asynchronous'... 'The pandemic accelerated many trends, from streaming, e-commerce, and food delivery platforms to the widespread adoption of remote work. But instead of taking advantage of this opportunity to improve how we work, most organizations simply took their offices online, along with the bad habits that permeated them.'

We didn't really have time to improve things; we just did what we could under most tricky circumstances. But here we are now, and we <u>can</u> do something about improving things.

Bad meetings are bad habits. Marcelo Lebre in 'Why you should be working asynchronously in 2022' from Remote.com says 'meetings are the most expensive tool your company has, use them properly'.

I agree. Don't use sync meetings for the majority of work... it's just too expensive.

Lynne Cazaly

Time is expensive. Why are we meeting?

Work is networked

Work is changing from sequential, step by step, do-it-in-this-order tasks, to more of a network or matrix.

There are different pieces to be done at different times by different people and we are all trying to orchestrate and coordinate things to bring them together and integrate them in a harmonious way, as best we can.

It's not perfect and it's not infallible. But if you've broken a big piece of work up, and sliced it into smaller bits and pieces, there's often a greater chance you'll tick something off from that list of work, and today! It's more easily delegate-able to others and it's more easily monitored, checked or tested by others.

We manage to bring a range of things together for a picnic involving a group or family. You bring the rugs, I'll bring the ice chest, you bring the smoked salmon, you bring the rain ponchos. Together we create a great piece of work. It's not on one person to do it all and if it is, it's probably an event worthy of other hands helping make the work lighter.

Then when we do come together in sync, our async efforts (baking, folding, preparing, packing, buying, driving, travelling, walking) all come together … in sync and in sync.

Lynne Cazaly

The Seven Conditions

'Work mentalities have shifted; people want work that fits in with their lives, not to arrange their lives around their work, which is how it used to be.' – The Age/Sydney Morning Herald

This quote is from *The Age* newspaper from my hometown Melbourne.

In 1990, I visited The Age newspaper in real life. It was a huge print processing and news headquarters located at the famous address of 250 Spencer Street in Melbourne, once described as a 'brutalist brown brick building'.

It was such a thrill, touring the editorial section, meeting the journalists, seeing the photo team processing and selecting images of the Australian Open tennis tournament that was in progress at the arena just a short distance away. Then we took a quick walk down a flight of stairs, down to the enormous printing press to hear the *thwack thwack thwack* of the paper rolls running through the press. There were operators at each of the huge metal rolls that held the imprints of the pages as they hit the paper with ink. We saw the paper cut and then magically ... it would drop out the bottom of the machine in a finished, hard copy, newsprint newspaper. We picked them up, fresh, the ink and pages feeling a little warm to the touch. Oooooh!

Everyone was in that same building. 100% co-located.

The sports reporters, the night editor, the print crew, the trucks were backed up to the loading docks and the drivers were waiting for their delivery to drop so they could drive out along the country roads of Victoria to deliver these first editions to early rising households, farmers and graziers.

So many people were on deck, live, in the moment, together, bringing the paper to life. And it was about 4am! Changes were being made to the stories, the headlines, the captions and the photos. The second edition then came out at about 4.30am and was bundled up and distributed around the city and suburbs.

A few years later the print and newspaper house moved to a bigger, brighter and newer facility on the fringes of the city. And then a little later, the media world changed dramatically and by far the majority of their readers were online. They needed neither the big space, the big printing press nor all of those staff on duty at the one time. Now they primarily work from a normal looking office in a normal looking building with a masthead lit up on the outside.

Work continues to change. And so must we.

Here are **7 conditions** to take notice of that are continuing to impact our changing world of work, and why we simply can't keep resisting the new but need to constantly adapt to it. Adaptability is the capability!

Condition 1: NOW

Real time is a thief

There are better ways of remote working. This we now know. It's clear that doing everything (or most things) in real time – that is you and me, now at the same time – is robbing us of progress. It's making things slower, harder, more complicated, frustrating and more d-r-a-w-n out.

Trying to find a common time when we can get together in real time can be so frustrating. And then when we do find that time, sometimes things change at the last minute. Their mother has to go into aged care, their child has a fever, they have to get the dog to the vet, they're snowed in and Wi-Fi is down, they're stuck in traffic, they had a health issue, they have to have a day off work.

Whatever that fundamental human need is, all of that prior waiting in the lead up to that in sync real time meeting is now wasted. Waiting for a real time anything is a thief of time, energy, momentum and motivation.

Condition 2: MEETINGS
Broken and unfixable

The belief we have that in just one meeting we could do ALL of the things on the agenda with ALL of those people here … is deluded.

Simply putting something on an agenda doesn't make it happen.

Meeting culture is broken, and no amount of social media posts, podcasts, books or training programs are fixing it quickly enough for the speed with which the world of work is evolving.

Harvard Business Review research surveyed 182 senior managers in a range of industries:

- 65% said meetings keep them from completing their own work.
- 71% said meetings are unproductive and inefficient.
- 64% said meetings come at the expense of deep thinking.
- 62% said meetings miss opportunities to bring the team closer together.

We'll have to do something else rather than meet.

Condition 3: WASTE

Throwing away so much

We needlessly waste hours and hours each week working in ways that are … wasteful.

A waste of time and energy, effort and engagement. It's a waste of electricity and resources, a waste of our mental and digital bandwidth, a waste of our attention and a waste of effort. How dare we drain our best people – including ourselves – by forcing them (us) to waste themselves (ourselves) away!

Calculate the time you say nothing and contribute nothing in that low value/no value meeting you're in today and you'll begin to quantify the tragic waste.

Plenty of organisations are finding better and easier ways to make progress and reach outcomes; let's learn from that.

Condition 4: KNOWLEDGE
Our need to know

We humans have a strong curiosity bias, so we are driven to continue to seek out information, and more and more and more of it. It's called 'maximising' and too much is never enough.

We're probably conditioned or addicted to wanting to hear it for ourselves too. How else could we know it was true? But knowing all this stuff: what difference does it make?

What if you didn't know?

'Wow, I didn't know that!' That's all you need to say (or preferably, think quietly to yourself) or 'I learned something today'. Some of us are affronted that we didn't know or weren't told. 'No one told me!' probably dates back to the Town Crier who would walk the streets ringing a bell and making announcements. They'd read the latest news out loud to the town folk. If you're still thinking today that no one told you, maybe there's another way for you to get that information.

There have been exclamations of 'I didn't know' or 'no one told me' for years. Research about employee communication in organisations often finds that staff 'want more communication'. I remember crafting the surveys that asked the questions that got those results! And I worked in the communications field!

More information. Perhaps that's why we cc and reply all

on our emails or invite 18 people to a meeting that goes for 3 hours when only 12 mins were relevant to 10 of the people.

We must break this addiction of 'needing to know'.

Given so much is find-outable with a Google search or a 'Hey, Siri', it's obvious that no, we do not need to know it all.

'Knowledge about' is not the measure of your worth and capability at work.

When we focus too much on whether we knew something or not we are setting up a standard or expectation that we will always need to know. It's quite addictive, not to mention that needing to know can become part of our role and identity.

There is no end to information. Sitting in status update meetings is pointless. Pointless I tell you! All of those individual updates can be logged and written and typed and scanned and read and heard and absorbed and mentally filed away in other async ways.

Condition 5: CONTROL
Pushing back on power

Team members and employees who followed the bouncing ball from here to there and back again (the workplace commute) are wanting to keep the flexibility they've enjoyed over recent years of zero commute... or less frequent commutes.

That means the 8am Monday morning project status meeting that was the bane of my existence in project team land is needed no longer. There are other ways.

I'm in Melbourne, Australia. An 8am start in New Zealand is 6am in Eastern Australia, and 4am in Western Australia and parts of Asia. It's the previous day - it's SUNDAY, they are out drinking, enjoying a Sunday sesh in Europe, UK and the USA! Don't bring them into a real time meeting... unless you're after a laugh and a virtual 'cheers' with rosy-cheeked, karaoke-singing revellers!

And no, we don't want to get up for a 4am meeting thank you. We'll stay under our snuggly warm duvet — which we can't even get out of if we wanted without disturbing three dogs and a cat. (Not entirely true for me; I'm petless at the moment).

People moving to regional locations of their choice, dropping kids at school, watching them swim or play sport or receive an award, or have tuck shop day. This is flexibility. Visiting my elderly parents and reminiscing through the photo albums over a cool drink and a piece of cake. This is flexibility. It's also a human desire and drive, a motivation. We want increased choice and flexibility. And I encourage you to push back on the control that may call for more sync work.

Condition 6: EXCESS

It's all too much

That BIG pack of information being presented and talked through in real time to everyone? Nope. No more please.

Unnecessarily complicated and convoluted; too many people; too big a task; too hard to do; too big a pack.

Stop 'presenting packs of information' in a real time sync meeting. It's a very 1990s thing to do. Presenting to everyone live, in real time and then talking through every line or every page is excessive. It's wasteful too.

It could singularly be the biggest element of wasted time in the business world, and likely learned from big consulting companies who do it to show they're spending client dollars on people, time and outputs that are visible.

The information being talked through and the big groups of people and all the hopes and dreams for that gathering; it's all too much. The chunks and wads of information are simply too big for people to deal with, cognitively process, make sense of, retain and recall.

Condition 7: BUSY

In-demand peoples

Waiting for busy people to 'get back to you' can slow progress to a stop.

Perhaps you're waiting for their expertise or their briefing or advice so you can begin. Maybe they're an important person, an in-demand person.

But you're still waiting to get access to them.

It's a huge delay factor, to be waiting for someone else to be available to join you in your-real time synchronous work.

There are backlogs and jammed-up pipelines of work everywhere that are resting with the people who are too busy, away on leave, having a morning at the dentist or working on another project.

Or maybe they're in another meeting!

Stop waiting for them and start working in a new way.

Why we sync so

It's interesting to see why and how we default to sync. Like biases and blind spots, you may not notice it until you read about it and then notice it!

It's a habit

We've been trained to work this way.

Think back to your first job. Who did you learn "work" from? The first organisations you worked in probably had ways of working that you followed, to fit in, to do your job well. We tend to adapt to the cultures and behaviours around us first, so that we fit in, before we start trying different things.

The habit of working in a way that defaults to sync – calling a meeting, working with someone else in real time, having a conversation, picking up the phone – is what many of us just do. How else could work be done but in the way we currently do it?

With new and agile ways of working sweeping the world over recent years, there are plenty of other ways to work.

And it's not all about productivity. There is a sensibility here, a greater personal preference and increasing choice and flexibility at work.

Trying to include

In all goodness, we also default to synchronous work because we try to include people, live, now.

- Do we worry that if they're not there, they aren't included?
- Do we only think that if a person is here with us, now, in real time, with everyone else, that is the only way we can include them?

Yet I can be live in a meeting, now, and still be discriminated against, mansplained, interrupted, excluded, minimised, forgotten, invisible, ignored and shut down.

It's not the synchronous work that is the issue; it's the biases, habits, defaults and behaviour of a culture that systematically excludes.

Winitha Bonney OAM, an expert in inclusion and diversity and a woman of colour with lived experience, speaks, trains and mentors on what we need to be doing differently. She says in Julia Steel's book 'Unite',

> 'It's great when organisations take a stance and act to create equity and equality. But more often than not, it's others making decisions on behalf of People of Colour. They may invite co-design, human-centred design, or consultation, but if the decision has not been made by us – if we have not had a seat at the table – then this creates supremacy, fragility and dominance. While the intent may be well-meaning, there are underlying psychological bonds of racism.'

We exclude people every day even when we think we're trying to include them.

We exclude via irrelevance, boredom and playing with our status. And we disrespect people's time and their preferences for when and how they like to work or when they are at their best.

Exclusion happens because too often the default way inclusion happens is 'you have to be there' – and that's a singular and old way of thinking and working.

To be excluded by unavailability – you couldn't make the live, in real-time time – doesn't pass anymore. It's not an excuse. There are other, better, newer and more inclusive ways to get input, engagement and participation from people and instead, to let them drive the work, to genuinely have a seat at the table, even if the table is an asynchronous one.

We think it's all important

Careful. Could we also believe that this work we're doing is so very important that it needs everyone there at once? And now!

And sure, that can be the case when there is a crisis or an urgent situation to resolve. But everyday work, no.

Not everyone needs to be there.

And less people need to be there than we think.

It's important work, yes, but not <u>that</u> important that such significant resources are expended to achieve such potentially insignificant outcomes.

We believe it's easier

We may believe it's easier to have everyone there at once. For the convener of the meeting or the leader of the work, it's absolutely easier, but the rest of us may have to sit through irrelevant conversations and content.

We may therefore think that other ways will be harder, that we will have to contact everyone individually 1:1 to get their input, ideas and comment or progress with the work. Or that we have to meet with everyone, singularly. That's not how this sync async thing works.

It could be easier to <u>not</u> have the meeting, workshop, interview or gathering in real time. At all. It could be easier to involve fewer people over a shorter stretch of time. In turn then, we may not have to do so much preparation for those 'big event' meetings or real time group work where there's so much that's going to happen. We tend to put more time and effort into projects or preparation when we believe that a lot is riding on it. Fewer big meetings could mean less of that perfection preparation.

And of course… what's easy for you could be neutral, inconvenient, frustrating, a complete waste or a $#@& nightmare for others. This is a great tool to use as a scale for measuring or rating a sync experience.

Here's a pic of it:

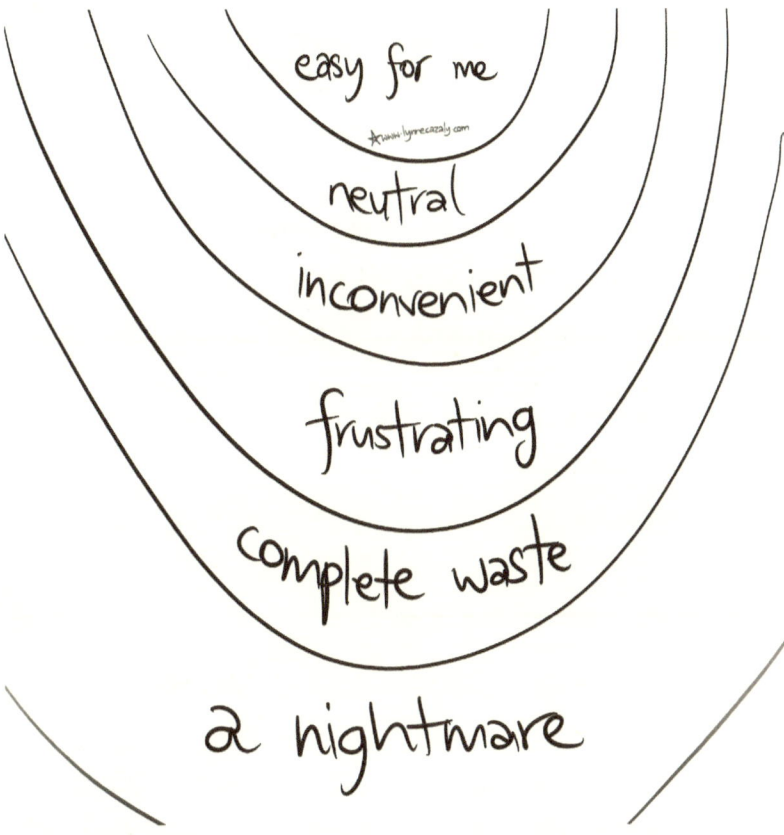

See the gap right here, to get out of this nightmare?

We may feel the need to see people in meetings and gatherings in real time.

'We need to be connected. And I need to be able to see their reactions so that I know that this stuff is landing and resonating with them,' said a team leader.

Yes, some people need the pressure of the performance, the audience in the live show, the deadline, the faces. But that could be about one person needing this. Check with the people in the team or group and they may think differently.

Sync work can sometimes be centred on only one person or a few people. It's **one** or **some**, not the **many**, **most** or **all** of the team or group.

'Great for one and can suck for many,' is how I like to think of it. The drive for increased synchronous work could have a downside for the many … even though it's great for the one.

And maybe something else…

There are many other reasons why we sync so.

- Perhaps we can't say 'no'. When a more senior leader or our boss requests a meeting with us or that we attend a sync gathering, it could be hard to say you want an asynchronous option. But it can be done and there's a section later in the book where I talk through how to do that, no matter the person, their position or status.

- Maybe we like, love and adore meetings, seeing each other and connecting and working in person in the moment. Maybe it's so much our preference that we simply don't want to work in any other way and the thought of not working in this way causes us to feel uncertain or disappointed about our future work.

- Potentially our job could be all about meetings,

interviews, conversations and synchronous work live in the moment.

- Maybe the organisation runs on meetings and catch-ups and get togethers so culturally, it's what's expected.
- And maybe it's something else…

The 3 Illusions of Synchronous Work

Before we switch on to more asynchronous work tools, methods and suggestions, consider what could be the biggest most valid reasons why we require or expect synchronous work.

I think they're illusions… because they may not be true.

1. The illusion of control

Hmmm, if I have you all here at once, then I am in control and we are a good team, because we are together. I can see what you are doing and I can see if you are engaged and I can see if you are contributing and therefore, I am managing and leading you.

Not so fast.

Maree Burgess in her brilliant book, 'Level Up: How managers learn to do less and be more' explains that being a control freak or having 'the need to control everything creates even more work.' She says letting go of this need to be across everything is part of the process of becoming a better leader.

If a middle level leader hasn't learned or been more formally trained in how to do what they do, there are great opportunities to try new ways. Burgess' description of shifting from a 'Transactional manager' to a

Transformational manager' is what the shift from too much sync work to more async work is all about too.

Shifting from, as she says:
- thinking there is only one way, their way;
- struggling to let go of doing everything; and
- disempowering the team.

The transformational manager is more of what asynchronous work needs. These managers and leaders:
- 'understand what they should be doing and what the team should be doing;
- can let go of the technical work and let their team get on with it;
- understand that there are different ways to achieve a result; and
- empower the team.'

Burgess says, 'learning to let go allows you to start to perform your role effectively, tap into your best thinking and help your team to thrive.'

Yes, thank you. That is progress.

2. The illusion of engagement

You're in an online meeting or catch up and you can see many, many people whose cameras are off.

People are online now, so they are connected somehow

to this team and the work. And they're adding things in the chat box and giving their feedback. So yes, there is some connection and engagement. But the mix of on and off cameras can lead us to think that those who are 'off' camera are disconnected and those whose cameras are 'on' are engaged.

But it's not that black and white.

Our delusion that people are engaged because we can see their face is rapidly losing validity. People can be highly engaged and yet we may not have seen them online or in person all day or all week. We may have been in contact with them asynchronously and collaborated with them, communicated and problem solved with them in other ways, at other times.

Be careful that your perception of what engagement is, isn't limited to someone's face being visible or you being able to see their facial expressions.

Delve further into building better cohesion and engagement by exploring the work of:

- Tracey Ezard in the book, 'Glue: The stuff that binds us together to do extraordinary work'
- Em Campbell-Pretty in the book, 'Tribal Unity: Getting from teams to tribes by creating a one team culture'.

Why the camera is off

We've probably been in remote meetings, presentations, workshops and sessions where people turn their cameras off.

Could the meeting be so slow and dull they say:

- *I'm eating*
- *My camera isn't working for some reason*
- *My background is messy*
- *My WIFI is unstable*

And yes, all of these can be true. Maybe we're paying 'continuous partial attention' and doing emails, emptying the dishwasher, cleaning up cat chuck or standing outside screaming in the rain because we've got so much to do.

Continuous partial attention is a concept coined by Linda Stone to explain the need to be included, tuned in, but doing multiple things at once. She says: 'In the case of continuous partial attention, we're motivated by a desire not to miss anything. We're engaged in two activities that both demand cognition. We're talking on the phone and driving. We're writing an email and participating in a conference call. We're carrying on a conversation at dinner and texting under the table on (our device).'

Hey, it's hard when a sync situation is so incredibly passive. Instead of making people wrong for not giving their full attention to a dull situation, change the way you do the work.

3. The illusion of progress

We are having lots of meetings, interviews, check ins and chats and there are lots of people in them, so it must be important, and we must be making progress. Aren't we? We've had six meetings so far and we are really making progress. Aren't we?

How do you know? Really know?

Dr Jason Fox in the book 'How to lead a quest' refers to the progress delusion. He says it's a state where we say 'yes' to so many little things, 'that the bigger, more important things suffer. It is insidious, pervasive and all too common. It afflicts all of us…and it requires a level of deliberation to lean against the flow of busyness, and say yes to the things that matter.'

Dr Fox's example is email and it's so relatable. 'You'll soon find yourself checking email and identifying small things to micromanage. Why? Because these things provide a rich and immediate sense of progress! Say you start your day with sixty emails in your inbox. By mid-afternoon, you've whittled your inbox down to fourteen. Ah! Progress! It feels like you're winning, and other people in the organisation know that you're putting in effort. Good work! No one can fault you.'

And it becomes part of how we 'do' work in the organisation and then 'reply all' is the norm, says Fox.

In the case of synchronous work - it's meetings that become the default thing we can't say 'no' to and I believe these become our daily and weekly sign of progress.

- *We had a meeting.*
- *I attended a meeting.*
- *They've scheduled a meeting.*
- *I've requested a meeting.*
- *We've got a meeting in two weeks.*
- *We're going to meet.*

Who hasn't thought, felt or said: 'I've had a day full of meetings! Phew! What a big one!' or 'We really made great progress today. It was back-to-back and I didn't have time for lunch, but I really think we might be finally getting somewhere.

Finally!? What the? All that time, effort, people and investment and we're *finally* getting somewhere?

Many of the meetings we've been in could have been examples of deluded progress. Compared to what Fox says is 'meaningful progress', doing the things that matter for the organisation. That is the harder work but the more meaningful.

We often want and need to gain access to people who are inaccessible, busy, booked out, pumped and stretched.

Progress gets stalled or thwarted by delays in simply trying to get all the right people in the right room at the right time.

This isn't about not getting people together at all; just save the effort of doing that for the meetings, conversations, interviews and workshops that really, truly count.

Don't struggle to find a time for say, 18 people to attend an online real time sync meeting and then let them sit passively looking at their screen while someone delivers a dry information pack of slides.

Oh, but it's interactive. I asked them do they agree.

It could have been an email with the deck attached. But it could also be likely to be ignored as being 'too big' or 'too heavy' to digest. We're already overloaded with information. I explored cognitive load coping in more detail in my book *'Argh! Too much information, not enough brain: A Practical Guide to Outsmarting Overwhelm'*.

Sync Async Tip

→ It could have been a video. And a short one. With adjustable speed. So I can see the slides, listen to the presentation and accelerate it, 1.5 - 2x the speed that it was delivered live.

All or pieces

Synchronous work can too often try to achieve everything in the one event. All at once.

versus

Asynchronous work dealing more frequently with pieces of work, over time.

And if we use both sync and async to progress our work, we get to take the best of synchronous work and add it to the most effective parts of asynchronous work.

Summary

It turns out that the option to choose more asynchronous work is better for me, you, them... and it, the work.

Those who need time to think can get it. Those who want to add their diverse thought to the work can give it. Opportunities for inclusion to grow across the team and organisation are available.

The effort we put into tasks and activities delivers a greater return than sitting silently in a listen-only mode sync situation.

We end up gaining greater control over our day and our role, instead of being side-tracked in lengthy inefficient meetings, conversations and gatherings.

Coming together in person, synchronously, can be saved for higher value, higher impact work. As Priya Parker explains in 'The Art of Gathering: How we meet and why it matters', 'We spend our lives gathering – first in our families, then in neighbourhoods .. schools.. then in meetings.. conferences.. product launches, board meetings... and we spend much of that time in uninspiring, underwhelming moments that fail to capture us, change us in any way, or connect us to one another.'

When you bring people together for low value/no value, low impact/no impact work, the outcome and purpose isn't clear, frustration rises and an individual's existing work pressures grow. Work satisfaction reduces and you've got other problems like retention, recruitment and failure to deliver your organisation's services.

Sync for high value and important stuff.

Async the rest.

Lynne Cazaly

PART 2

Where do we go from here?

Lynne Cazaly

Introduction

Don't just flick the switch overnight announcing, 'we're all going async now; no more sync anything', but rather extend what you're already doing and find opportunities for more asynchronous work in place of wasteful sync.

Identify and notice synchronous work that's wasteful when it happens, when you're invited to it or when you're in the thick of it.

Use the guidance that follows to help you shift individually and as a team.

Lynne Cazaly

A variety of people – a variety of ways

When we know no other way of working or we're just trying to survive our workload, considering new ways of doing things seems out of left field and too hard.

For some people working in teams, they find the way they're currently working a familiar and safe structure. It could be a way they've always worked. Why change?

Some workplaces prescribe how to work; 'you need to do it this way!' Exerting power and force for compliance.

It can seem easier to just give in and follow those rules; after all, it might be a 'the devil you know' situation.

For those keen to achieve more, this could be the kind of change in work and career you've been looking for. It's already somewhat familiar and you can bring more of it to your conscious awareness.

Many teams working in this way feel an immediate release of pressure. It pulls them together as a team, because they are making choices for themselves and allowing their colleagues to make choices too. Can you feel that? The push and pull of power are diminished.

More evolved teams and workplaces accept that we need to work in a variety of ways if we're to live well. There is choice, freedom and flexibility at the front of many decisions that people make. Don't believe it? Wait a while and you'll see good people departing to work with teams, leaders and organisations where more strategic sync async is just how they do things.

It's all about progress... and trust

In 'The Power of Small Wins', by Teresa M Amabile and Steven J Kramer, the authors say, 'the power of progress is fundamental to human nature, but few managers understand it or know how to leverage progress to boost motivation.'

Seems we've been missing the power and reward of small steps, small wins and little pieces of progress.

They go on to say, 'Of all the things that can boost inner work life, the most important is making progress in meaningful work.'

Instead of sync work potentially slowing progress or stopping it all together at times, async has the capacity to boost and accelerate our progress.

Marcelo Lebre in 'Why you should be working asynchronously in 2022' from Remote.com says async is 'a way for workers to organise the order in which tasks are executed to align with their own timetable'.

And communication 'is not expected to be immediate'. This leads to the opportunity to 'fine-tune work' which helps reduce pressure on everyone!

In short, it means if we're on the same team, we don't all have to be online at the same time. We can work on things without waiting for others.

That means we're making progress.

But it's also not just about going off and doing your own thing all the time. One of the keys, as Lebre explains, is 'creating processes that allow employees to work autonomously and providing employees with the trust they need to do so'.

Dan Pink referred to autonomy in his wildly popular book 'Drive: The surprising truth about what motivates us' and the three surprising things that motivate us are: purpose, mastery and autonomy. Ding ding ding Dan! (Hey, read his most recent book on 'Regret' – you could save yourself plenty… I regret being in so many meetings!)

Trust is a big part of async work.

In contrast - stark, often slow and painful contrast - synchronous work ties our progress to communication and collaboration among teams. Because one person is unavailable, progress slows, stalls and often stops, until they're back from leave or until they can finish something else and join us. Decisions don't get made, content doesn't get created and progress isn't achieved.

Of course, not all the time. But often enough that makes progress slow to a crawl.

Async work is like how hotel cleaning happens.

Someone knocks on the door for room cleaning.

Someone else for room service or meal delivery.

And usually someone else knocks and shouts 'mini baaarrrrrrr!'

When to sync async

'Two hours I was in a meeting. Two. The only thing I did was put my virtual hand up to agree to something. And put a smiley face in the chat box. What a waste. And they wonder why I turn my camera off.'

This quote is from a team member in a mid-sized organisation and its indicative of many of our experiences.

The best time to consider choosing to work in more async ways is before even starting a new or fresh piece of work.

The second-best time to consider working in async ways is during sync experiences that aren't working.

Here's how it can go:

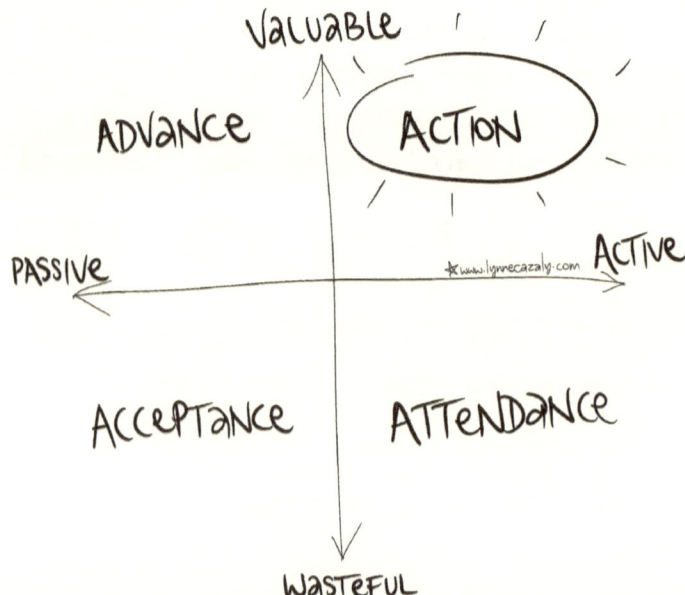

Work is wasteful or valuable ... or somewhere in between

It's a question to ask yourself: is this VALUABLE? Is what I'm doing right now a valuable use of my time, valuable in terms of achieving the outcome and getting the results I need to achieve, valuable for what it is?

And if you're not sure, work from the other angle of waste. Ask yourself: is what I'm in right now WASTEFUL, wasteful in achieving the outcome, wasteful for what it is?

We can all tolerate some waste here and there; but when it's extreme, excessive or repetitive, there's an opportunity right there to reconsider how you're working.

Are you just sitting there in ACCEPTANCE mode, tolerating this?

Work is passive or active ... or somewhere in between

To help you work out if it's wasteful or valuable, check how active or how passive you are.

We've all been in a meeting, conversation, session or situation with others where we're passive. And that's ok; if it's valuable. Perhaps we are quietly listening or observing. Maybe that's our role. To be a witness, observer, supporter or silent advocate or ally. I see this as work that is helping ADVANCE something; an idea, a cause, a strategy, a vision, a change, a culture.

Most other synchronous experiences though, rise exponentially in value when we are actively involved. When there is ACTION. We're participating, contributing, engaged and are part of the fabric of what is being created, or co-created.

And still, not all activity is valuable. Have you been a participant in a workshop session where you did plenty of mindless activities that had no link to the outcome, no purpose for engagement and connection and seemed to just be a time-filler to give the facilitator a bit of a break? I sure have! So that's a big 'no' from me. Not valuable and most certainly wasteful even if I was active. I'd call that in ATTENDANCE.

And we can allow passivity, silence, observation… when it contributes to the outcome or the valuable process that is underway. It doesn't need to be a gym workout or an over-the-top party!

If it's the default – that everyone comes together at the same time so we can all listen to two people talk something out, then no.

It could have been async.

I could have read the transcript or watched the video.

I could have asked for a 90-second summary from a colleague who attended the sync thing.

As soon as you're passively observing you can think, 'OK, it could potentially be an async piece of work.'

- You could watch the recording.

- Read the pack prior or post the meeting.
- Send your notes via chat.
- Read or search the transcript later.
- Add your thoughts to a shared document. (And if there isn't one yet, then be the person who creates one.)
- Send a message to a colleague about what else you think.
- Vote or give detailed feedback via a survey or form.
- And yes, check in with a colleague who was there about what happened.

You don't have to be there for two hours. As soon as you're passively observing … get the heck outta there!

Then when we are in active participation in sync work, there is stuff for us to do! Listen. Think. Pause. Reflect. Write a note. Contribute. Take a break. Have a conversation. Share a story. Add to a shared document and watch it grow before our very eyes! Job done. There's little to no time to be bored and be distracted to look at our emails or check social media on our device. We're actively participating in the synchronous work, in real time, in the now. That's valuable and worth contributing to.

It's safer, better, easier

There is a power in sync work. But continuing to default to working in this way doesn't just have problems of inefficiency or ineffectiveness as I've spoken about so far.

Many of us would have experienced the power that's present in meetings.

As a facilitator for over 15 years, I've worked with hundreds of teams and groups, helping them make progress and work well together.

And in every group, every single time, there are always power dynamics at play. Status, power, influence, pressure, coercion, politics — they're all there.

It's in the way someone looks at another; or the muffled sound they make; the remark; the tone of their voice; the words they use; the frustration they express; their body language; their facial expressions; their attitudes; their behaviour… it is all there.

And all these things can have a detrimental effect on how safe people feel to express what they think.

In so many workshops I've facilitated, the most senior person in the organisation - the Managing Director or the Chief Executive Officer or Chair of the Board, and often all three - would be in attendance. And you can see people close themselves up, clam up and shut down. They're just not willing to be as open and frank and relaxed with their ideas, input and contributions. They're not.

As a facilitator, I'll use a range of techniques throughout the session to make the status and power clear and visible, to not try to hide it. But I'll also help those senior leaders with the management and delivery of their ideas and power. AND help those who may not have felt safe in their presence, build up to feeling safer and safer as the session progresses.

I know many people don't consider this an issue because it's not a problem for them. And this is the bias of power.

To say 'just speak up' or to ask 'why didn't you say so in the meeting' shows a lack of understanding about psychological safety.

Consider how you will gain people's input, engagement, participation and contribution — before, during and after — a synchronous, in real time meeting.

Because async can be safer.

For people with disabilities, the opportunity and possibility for remote and async work has been life-changing and life-enhancing. To be able to work at a time of day or night that works for you. To work for as long as what suits you. To use tools, methods or applications that make things easier for you is liberating. Choices become greater, and independence and agency are enhanced.

Artefacts of actuality

It can be hard to shift out of more sync work and not have everyone come together, particularly when clever people are involved.

When we need someone in the room because they know the history or situation or background, then there are other issues at hand.

What if they leave? And they will. What if they are ill or have an accident? Or die. And it happens.

When history is housed in people, it makes losing the memory of the organisation like this a real risk. The 'Farewell! We'll miss you' card could be edited to say, 'Farewell! We'll miss what you know about this joint!'

This is how work has truly shifted for Baby Boomers and Generation X-ers working in businesses where the documentation was stored in their brains. So little information was stored anywhere else that was accessible. Filing cabinets dammit! Crystal tabs. Suspension files. If you know what I'm talking about, you know. If you don't, then you are so hot for async.

I did some university work experience at Melbourne's radio station FOX-FM. There I was, so freakin excited, facing five full days in radio heaven. I had a day in each aspect of the station: the newsroom, the on-air studio, the production workshop, the music library and administration/management.

Right away on day one I had the opportunity to help

prepare the 10am news bulletin. 'Rewrite this,' said the news reader journalist, Helen. It was about traffic delays on the morning commute on the South Eastern Freeway. 'Check with the news reporter Jay, she said, 'does he have any actuality for the car accident that happened on the freeway this morning.'

Any what? Actuality? Yes, the reality, something from the real event. Not a crushed fender or broken glass but an interview, a sound bite, a live or pre-recorded report from the scene or a chat with the road clean-up crew or the police. This was the actuality she was looking for that she could include in the bulletin and help make the news more engaging, accurate and informative. It was the real, the actual stuff from the actual event.

I think this was the time I realised the true value of artefacts. The actuality of them. Artefacts are things made by humans and they often have cultural and historical significance. We tend to think they belong in a museum or art display – like a shield, ancient carving, weapon or food preparation tool.

Human-made artefacts are an important part of today's workplace, but we don't use them nearly enough.

As we move to more and more asynchronous work, artefacts made by the humans we work with will become even more important. They will hold threads of knowledge, show the path and evolution of our thinking, document decisions and capture ideas and be the reality from history.

They will be artefacts and records of cultural history in the organisation. And they will be representations of real life, artefacts of actuality.

We need to shift from the evolution and genesis of a project or piece of work residing in a human brain. When they leave to start their own consulting business, that knowledge goes too.

I recall my father Noel, during his career as a mechanical engineer, lecturer and teacher, saying when a colleague left the college, 'a whole lot of history just walked out the door. We've lost it. The history of this place is walking around in people'.

It's like how we might grasp on to the stories of our elders - parents and grandparents - to understand what it was like, what happened, who was who and how it impacted them. More actuality.

Just as we crave actuality and artefacts – stories, books, certificates, letters, diaries – from our history, so does an organisation. Too often we don't know we need it until it's too late.

To function effectively, we need to know what happened. And if we can search an historical record system in the business, accessible to all, not just a senior few, then we have greater access to find out what we need without interrupting people or putting the onus on them to tell us. We'll be more likely to be able to seek and discover for ourselves.

Async work can give you time to access actuality and artefacts as well as create them. When we sync and work together, if we create actuality from that, we make sync async work easier and make progress easier too.

Growing thoughts and ideas

It's challenging to be put on the spot in a meeting or workshop, particularly when there's an expectation you'll just magically come up with brilliant ideas. Growing great thoughts and ideas can take time.

Working async can help you grow more ideas. It gives people more opportunities, time and space to think.

Plus, if you give yourself a night's sleep in that time, you'll come up with even better ideas, and more of them! Our brain loves to do a bit of sorting and synthesis overnight as well as filing, processing, mixing and taking out the trash.

If there's a meeting or workshop you've got coming up and it's about generating ideas, put your brain to work on the task sooner.

You don't need hours of actual thinking time; it's elapsed time that can help.

It will give you more chances to:

- connect different things,
- keep a look out for existing ideas to combine into new ideas,
- find themes, topics and subjects to join together, and
- be exposed to more sources of inspiration.

You don't have to be in a meeting, interview, workshop or other kind of sync situation to come up with an idea.

How to do it async?

- observe, think and progressively make notes about your thoughts **before** the meeting
- add to those notes about your thoughts that come up **during** the meeting
- keep adding to your notes **after** the meeting.

Each of these situations has the potential to help you grow plenty of ideas. Start planting sooner.

Get out of their way

That quote about hire good people and then get out of their way… I'm not *usually* a fan of it because I've believed people may need to be assisted or facilitated through various stages of work.

But yes, of course, we also need to be given the ability, freedom and choice to work independently. This is where I'm shifting my thinking and looking at how asynchronous work can work where facilitation may have previously had a hand.

You do get out of people's way. Set some stuff up and then step aside.

Here's how:

- Leave them to do some work. Alone.
- Give them some space to gather some momentum.
- Allow them some 'clear air' to think and work.

On the topic of 'clear air', for 15 years I sailed with my father, Noel, on the beautiful waters of Port Phillip in Melbourne in sailing dinghy classes known as Pacers and Tasers. At the start of the race each week, the starting line would be a flurry of boats, sails flapping in the wind and disturbing the air in the area. We'd try to swiftly set a course to get out of that 'dirty air' and get some speed up.

Even if it wasn't the perfect tactical or positional decision in terms of the layout of the course, the decision was to go for clean air. Aaaaah, the beauty of undisturbed or turbulent air. Once we were in it, weeeeeeee - we would fly along. Strong, clear, consistent wind flow across the sails. It was MAGIC!

It's the same principle in a plane; clean air is wonderfully smooth. Bumps and turbulence are simply signs of dirty air, disturbed air from changing weather systems, wind from another direction or generally unsettled conditions like the build-up before a storm. Pilots are always in touch with air traffic controllers on the route (I know this, I hear this because I listen to ATC – yes, totally an #avgeek) seeking 'ride reports'. They want to know what other pilots have reported about the conditions along the route. Soon enough, a plane experiencing some dirty air at 29000 feet will be cleared to go up to 30000 feet or 31000 feet to see if it's smoother up there. They might go down to 28000 or 27500 feet too.

Turbulence gets categorised across six levels of disturbance or 'chop'. I use this scale to help me think about the disturbance I'm feeling with work and how 'disturbed' the air around some work is:

1. Light chop
2. Light turbulence
3. Moderate chop
4. Severe turbulence
5. Extreme turbulence.

Go for more opportunities for clear air, light chop. You'll have clearer and smoother space for better thinking. And you'll rest up ready for the sync situations if they have a lot going on or you experience moderate chop in a tough or tricky meeting. Hopefully there's no severe or extreme turbulence. That's when you've got that messy situation of everyone talking/disrupting/debating versus the clean air opportunities of asynchronous work. Smoother. Nicer ride.

Hey, most of us don't like turbulence even though planes are built to withstand it. That's a little bit like synchronous work. We may not like many of the flow on effects of more and more sync meetings, but we tend to be able to stand it or handle it.

To shift into smoother air of async work, we may need to become greater collators, collectors or curators of input from people prior to or after sync situations.

It's important then to consider how involved people will be in your sync and async gatherings … and work generally.

How involved

Before you go all sync and call a meeting, send out an invite or ask someone if they 'have two minutes', decide what you're trying to do.

Consider how involved people need to be across the work and what you're trying to do by working with others.

I've written about this thinking in my book, 'Create Change: How to apply innovation in an era of uncertainty'.

The idea with this is you identify how involved you need people to be and then work in accordance with that depth.

I wrote:

> "You may want them fully empowered. Or perhaps this is about some consultation. Or something else. At each step or stage of work, keep asking yourself questions like:
>
> - Is this a briefing or transfer of information? (**inform**)
> - Is it a consultative thing - I want to ask some questions and find out what they think? (**consult**)
> - Do I need to involve them in the design or development of a process, product or service? (**involve**)
> - Is it about collaboration: 'let's work on this

thing together'? (**collaborate**)

- Do I want them to pick up the ball and run with it, to empower them so that they act and decide? (**empower**)

Whichever of these you'd like to make happen – and you may want to achieve several on one piece of work – you need to be clear, otherwise it leads to confusion, greater uncertainty and mixed messages.

Here's a continuum or scale that can guide you. Get your goggles on: how low do you wanna go?

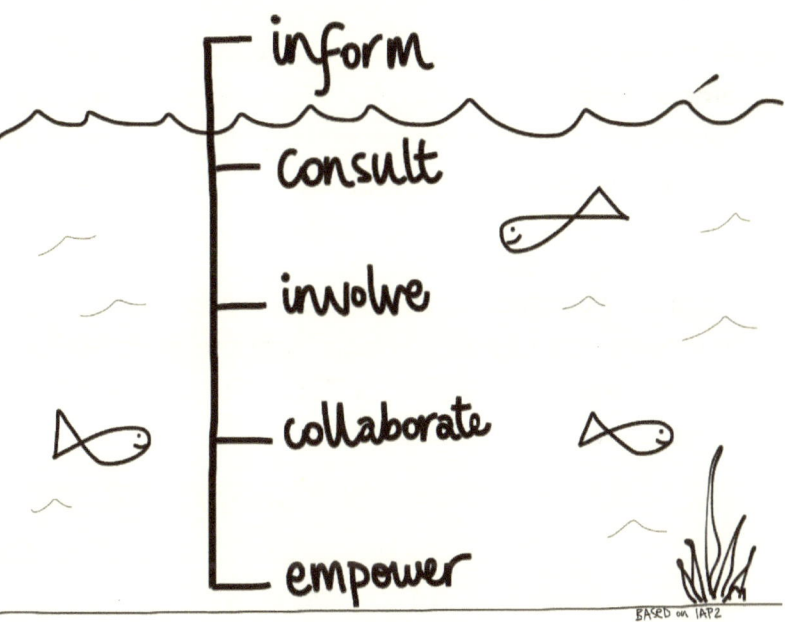

Based on the International Association of Public Participation (IAP2) continuum of participation

Informing people .. is very much on the surface. You tell them, they listen. You all move on.

But you can go further. When you **consult** with people, you're getting under the surface, you're asking them what they think, you want their views and those views may well impact the shape and size of things to come.

To go deeper is to **involve** people. How do they see things? What would they do? What do they think needs to happen? Get their ideas, their thoughts, their ways of thinking and seeing and bring them into it.

Oh, yes you can go further. To **collaborate** with people, you go deeper. 'Co' means to work together. Now you're talking, listening, meeting, co-creating, co-designing and co-delivering this thing together.

And even further you can go where people are **empowered** to design, create, deliver or implement ... Give them power, decision making, financial, resource, timing: it's theirs for the making.

I regularly use these five levels and 'depths' of involvement and participation (adapted from the International Association for Public Participation, or IAP2) to guide me in:

- how to prepare for engaging with a team,
- how to set up and design an environment a team is going to meet or work in,
- what processes they'll work through when I'm facilitating a meeting or workshop, and
- how to handle the stuff that happens during that team's meetings, work, conversations and

projects.

What you do as a leader makes a b-i-g difference in how well a group or team goes towards achieving an outcome.

And how you set the scene is super important. It's not 'their fault' or 'up to them'. It's on you. If you've called a meeting, are facilitating a workshop, leading a piece of work or responsible for getting the outcome, it really helps to get clear about what you're going to do and when and how you'll engage them to make something good happen.

Just as a trained scuba diver plans their dive, maps out the use of their oxygen supplies and prepares their equipment, leaders too need to plan the depth of involvement and engagement with their teams, colleagues and stakeholders."

This works so well with sync async work too. You can choose different elements of the work and decide or assess how involved people will be, and then whether the work will be best done sync or async ... or a combo.

It really is a BIG one. So much information and communication is intended for one way only. The only thing we perhaps want to do is ensure people understand. But even that invites other ways to communicate and work than going default to a real time meeting.

And then we might want to collaborate and involve

people in deeper aspects of the work, but not all of it... all the time.

Collaboration is possible and does occur at different times. We can still have collaborated on a book. An editor of a book doesn't work at the same time as the writer. It's after the writing. Same with the design and layout. It's done later. Identifying the pieces of work that can be async-ed is key here.

What absolutely needs to be done now, live at the same time? That's the sync work.

A quick chat

When Fiona emailed me seeking 'a quick chat' - that was the title of the email - about book publishing, I knew we could be headed for sync. I async-ed (emailed) back to find out what she needed to know. She didn't know what she needed to know, yet. And so, this revealed that the quick chat could have become one of those 30-minute conversations or a two-hour consultation, as we try to work out what we need to know.

I could have said, 'sure' and locked in a time for later that day to have that quick chat or even had the chat right then. But that right there is the problem with doing work immediately. Why do I have to do it now?

As it unfolded over the next three or four days, I never ended up in sync or spoke with Fiona. I replied and we had an insightful email exchange of information, and it was all async work. She was after **information**; that first level of the depth gauge from a few pages earlier. She wanted to learn more. There was no decision for us to make, there was no collaboration to be done. And it was information that a Google search may have revealed.

And here's what happens; many of us ask others to find out information. And that's ok. But the receiver of the request doesn't always have to go into real time sync to answer the question. It's not being rude. It's protecting our time and mind and space and life.

The result of this request was that I spent about 8 minutes across 4 emails giving Fiona key information, once I'd uncovered what her specific question was.

It's too easy to be drawn into the entanglement and involvement when it may not be to your advantage. We may have ended up talking about everything and anything, across a wide range of topics.

But wouldn't it have been nice to connect with her and speak with a human?

Yes, and it wasn't the focus of my work at that time.

Remember to focus on **the work** to be done.

Consider **how** it can be achieved without everyone all at once.

Eight minutes async across a couple of days versus an unknown time sync.

What is your preference?

Do you know what your preference is regarding how you work... and do you ask for it, push for it or express it?

Your working preference can quickly identify why some types of work are good and flowing for you and other types are frustrating or feel like you're not getting anywhere.

Understanding how others work can be helpful for us too. It helps keep progress happening and sustains great working relationships.

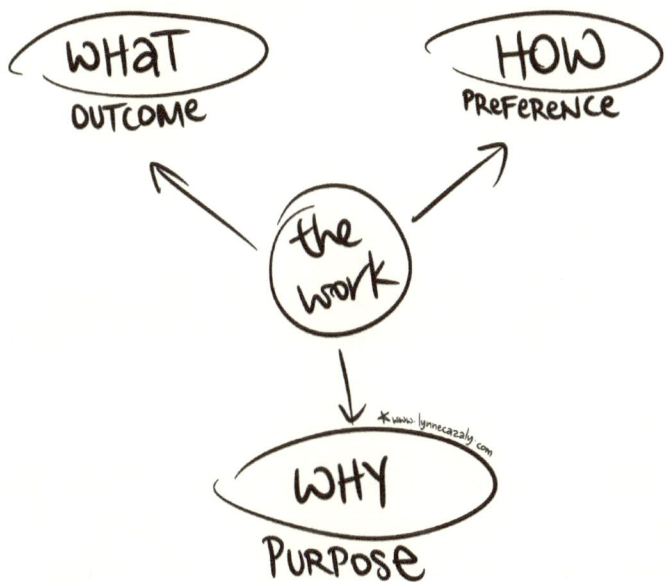

When we look at **the work** to be done, it's vital to understand **why** we're doing it – the **purpose** – and the **what** we're doing – the **outcome**. But remember to also consider **how** you'll do it – the **preference** or way of working.

Let's say you and I were going to work on a project or task together. How would you like to do that? What's your **how** … you're preferred way of working? That is, if there were no rules, what would you do?

Would you:

- Get things started independently?
- Wait until there was a kind of guide or framework for the work set up and then get working?
- Step in and out as needed throughout, to add your expertise and help advance things along?
- Drip feed your contributions at all stages and phases?
- Wrap things up and finish it off?

Or all of these? Or something else, some other way of working?

It's worth asking people what their preferences are; it can also help you work out what yours are when you see them in action.

When I'm working with a team helping them work more consciously in sync async ways or helping them through the transition to new and creative ways of working, I'll keep a look out and observe how people are behaving, working, thinking and talking.

Just as these following **four ways of working** can be human behaviours, they can also be stages of sync async work – I use them every day when working with a team or group:

- Initiator
- Contributor
- Advancer
- Completer

Think also of a piece of work starting, and going through these stages to the finish:

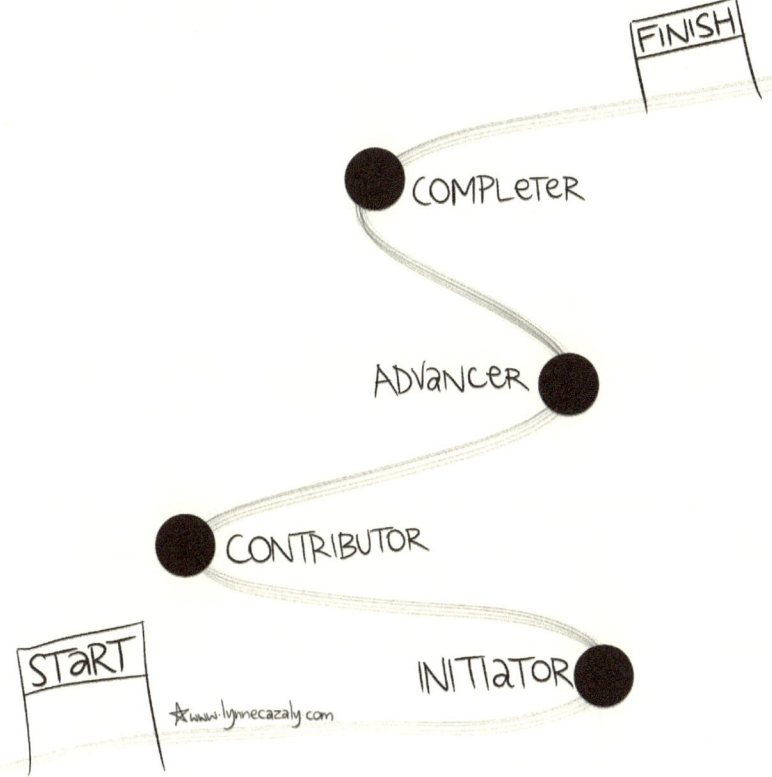

Let's look at them individually:

INITIATOR

Are you or are they an initiator?

Think ignition, starting a fire, getting flame, pouring energy into something to kick it off, begin it or launch it. Instigators and initiators in organisations and teams are truly wonderful. While many people may have spoken about something – you know, 'we should do something about that', or 'we really need to fix that for our customers' – initiators find the key steps that are needed and they get it going.

They help get a piece of work or project out of a state of stop, out of inertia and into motion, movement and momentum. And once that's happening, it's all go! Anything is possible.

Praise the initiators. And it's ok if they step aside after that; after all, they've done an important thing getting it going.

An initiator I've observed is Lisa Messenger of Collective Hub. Entrepreneur, author, serial starter of things, a mega-instigator, she demonstrated it clearly during the floods crisis in New South Wales in Australia in early 2022. Observing her ignition efforts on social media was incredible: rallying people, finding out what was needed where, gathering lists of needs, deciding on locations and support. A true starter.

CONTRIBUTOR

Are you or they a contributor?

People's contributions – good, bad, relevant or irrelevant – help keep the energy and momentum building with progress. It's a vital part of building interest and making forward steps in something.

If something has started and is up and going, even in the early days, think about how to get people to contribute to keep it going. And do you need to do that in real time or async?

Many leaders and organizational cultures do this sync by default. They hold a meeting with 18 people on the call and there's one person asking for ideas and contributions. But it can be hard work or near impossible to get brainstorming happening when you need it.

In the 1990s I worked in the public health sector and as part of my role in Community Relations, we raised funds for the health service to buy vital equipment the Government didn't fund. When we'd run a fundraising campaign with a big target – say, a $200,000 campaign or even a bigger $1,000,000 campaign – we wouldn't announce or launch the campaign until it was already underway.

This was one of the key theories of fundraising: that people will give more when they see the target is achievable, reachable and that – via social proof, other people are giving – it's a safe and smart thing to do.

The same will happen in making progress asynchronously.

With contributors to your tools, techniques, methods and processes, you'll drive more interest ... and in turn, more contributions, which leads to making more progress.

Later I'll share specific tools for sync async work and when it comes to gathering contributions – say on a shared visual collaboration board – having more than a blank canvas to start with is helpful. It boosts other contributions.

ADVANCER

Are you or they an advancer?

Early contributors to the work have made their contributions and you've now got to keep this thing going.

This is the heart of work. It is working through what can be the tough stuff, the boring stuff, the middle that is messy or the greatest parts of unknown territory.

How do you get people to advance the work? Does it need to be synchronous or asynchronous or is it and, both?

What is the best way to keep getting progress and to keep advancing the work?

Touching into and away from synchronous to asynchronous and back again is the one of the ways.

It probably won't *just* be one or the other. Think about:

- What do people need?
- What is the process you will use to get progress happening?
- What work needs to be done?
- What is the next step? And how should we do that?

What is the best and/or the easiest way?

COMPLETER

Are you or they a completer?

Making progress, getting contributions, advancing the work. At some point we're going to need to finish and complete this task or project.

Some pieces of work seem to fritter away or taper off and get forgotten. Perhaps they're not needed anymore. No problem. But if they are, who is the completer that is driven, motivated and strengthened by completing tasks?

- What needs to be done?
- Who are the people?
- What is the process?
- What is the work that you will do?
- What is the way that you will do this finishing work?

For example, if a piece of work needs to be completed, do 16 people need to be on a call, all at once? Or could three people meet to generate the ideas and actions and then go and do the work? Could they liaise through the greater group in more asynchronous ways?

Warning: The joy of initiators is starting stuff. At this stage, they might find some more stuff to start and begin digging some rabbit holes to dive into! It could be good, creative and innovative. But it could be distractingly not good.

Sam, a colleague I worked with used to like tasks done to about 80% completion. They'd add a little magic dust on top and the thing would be done. They might change the name or the description or the summary or add something to the whole thing that would take it to the next level. They were a true completer, taking things through that final finishing ribbon to the end.

But starting things? Nope. Not them. Don't meet with Sam with a blank sheet of paper. Not their thing. They'd ask, 'what have you already done? Where are you at?'

Not an initiator or instigator but certainly a contributor, usually later in the process. Sam trusted whatever had been done up until that point was good enough. They trusted that people had done the best they could with what they had, and they never set to try and re-engineer or re-work the work. Just a sprinkle of Sam's magic and the task, piece of work or project would be done, building on all the work done prior by many others.

Don't doubt that you can still co-create using async work: it is all about acknowledging that people work in different ways. We can all work on different things in different ways at different times and on different stages of a piece of work.

With sync async work, you can initiate something, give it to some contributors, hand it over to advancers and wrap it up with the completers.

When the work comes to you

Keep a look out for the delays and hold ups that can slow things down or act as obstacles or bottlenecks to making progress.

I'm not saying you need to send a message saying, 'Hey, now Jem, you're holding things up' but you might simply **notice** where things are being held up and know that's where you can apply some pressure.

Holds ups, hold ons and hand offs are key things I like to consider.

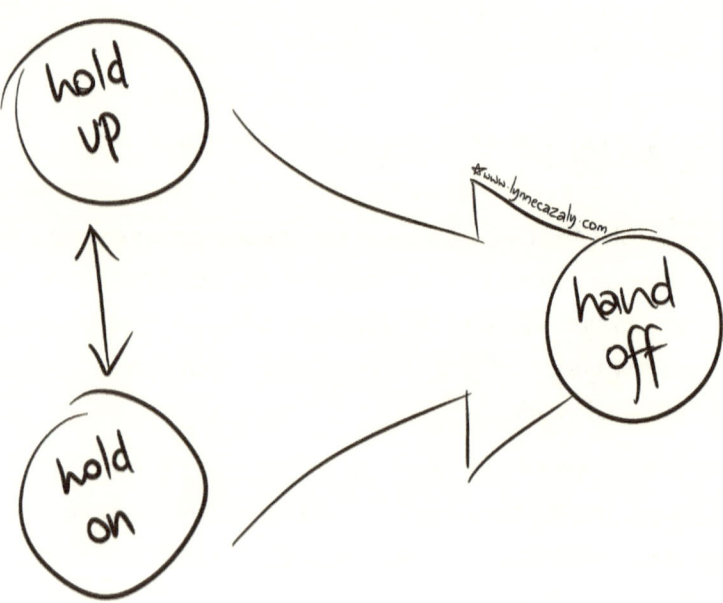

Holding Up

This will be like a dam wall. A heap of tasks or project pieces are all bunched up, waiting. Waiting for someone to come back from leave, waiting for them to be available, waiting for something to be signed off. This is a brilliant opportunity to find out how you can release the pressure that's holding up progress.

It could be that it's an old system they are following or an old process that just takes a long time.

A few years ago, I worked with Australia Post and after a Kaizen (continuous improvement) session we looked at how the team were able to reduce the sign on for a corporate account from 18 days down to 3. Phew! The team found all the ways to make things keep moving along.

But waiting? It can be one of the biggest wastes of time, effort, energy and resources. And brand.

When things are held up – say, waiting for responses from other people, departments, authorities, decision makers, systems or tools – we waste.

We delay progress.

We reduce momentum.

We invite inertia.

We tempt disengagement.

Holding On

If someone's 'holding on' to work, tread gently. One of the topics I explored a few years ago was that of perfectionism. In my book 'ish: The Problem with our Pursuit for Perfection and the Life-Changing Practice of Good Enough' I uncovered how perfectionists will often hesitate to show or share first drafts as they'll want to keep working on things until they are better, better, better... perfect. In their eyes.

But this reliance on only their perception of the quality and standard is both wasteful and dangerous. Perfectionism has dire effects for how we feel about ourselves and how our health outcomes can play out. Holding on to things because 'they're not finished yet', could reveal that:

- the task is too big
- the standard is unclear
- the quality required is too high

… or some other situation that might benefit from a few people breaking it down and getting through it.

I was reading Greg Jacobsen's KaiNexus blog on lean and continuous improvement. In lean manufacturing – think The Toyota Way production management system that Toyota follows to make cars – it might be called 'over processing'. It's doing more work than is required. It might be best to just stop where you are and see what else is required rather than trying to do more and more in an effort to make it perfect.

Handing Off

Yes, this is great. Do your bit and hand it along to others in the team, crew, project or collaboration. Get your bit done. Others may be waiting on it. The metaphor of a relay race has been used to describe asynchronous work; we may work on part of something before someone else gets their hands on it.

I was at the Melbourne Formula 1 Grand Prix event over the weekend and went up to the bar to get a refreshment. They were 'waiting on' the delivery cart from another location to bring more stocks of drinks. Within seconds, a team member dashed through the side door and handed over six bottles of champagne. Cheers!

Your mobile device will hand off to your laptop or desktop if they're connected or on the same network and you can shift frequently from one to the other. It's like your task can go on uninterrupted from one device to another. And cellular phone networks hand off from one tower to the next to make sure your phone call or browsing is uninterrupted from your mobile device.

I noticed it's also how cricket commentators hand off to the next batch of commentators during a broadcast; they're not ALL required on air, all at the same time.

If things are slowing or stalled, stay alert. Something might need handing off. Even part of the work handed off means others can get started on their piece.

Keep a look out for signs that things need to be

dislodged or moved gently or gradually along through the phases of progress:

- Does it need a bit more initiator?
- Is greater contribution required?
- Would an advancer help things progress?
- When does a completer need to step in?

Think about the way you're doing the work.

- What async work might help?
- Is a sync situation or experience needed?

We may expect perfect everything: perfect meetings, projects, reports and data and be frustrated when it's not a smooth and perfect run. Like wanting all the traffic lights to be green. But things aren't quite like that.

There are opportunities to help things through asynchronously. In other words, you don't need to 'get everyone in a meeting' to find out what's going on. OMG please don't default to this.

Perhaps a question in chat or a message to ask where the obstacles are.

Or the short daily stand-up meeting - a ritual from agile ways of working - asks team members what they're working on and what the perceived or actual obstacles are. This flags the blockers as something that might need some more attention or some more hands on the work.

Involved or Untangled

Working sync async can lead you to:

- **Involve** yourself further, deeper into work that is relevant and valuable for your role; or

- **Untangle** or remove yourself from work that is irrelevant, repetitive, wasteful or of no/low value.

Too often our default behaviour is to 'go along' with the call for more synchronous work, and so we get more and more involved in it.

Meeting requests and invites are a prime example.

We're invited to meetings and workshops that share no clear purpose, agenda, timings, process or outcome — and we stay in meetings that are passive, boring, time wasting, uninspiring and poorly led.

But when we decide to do more of our work asynchronously, we can ask for and clarify details — to determine whether we need to actually be at that meeting. More on this soon in the techniques section.

Anyway… it's no longer about fixing meetings.

Working in more asynchronous ways can help us untangle from wasteful, repetitive and low value work.

We can choose to contribute in other ways — prior to or post a meeting or use tools, methods and apps to work in different ways.

If you've wondered 'how did I ever get caught up in this?', it's a sure sign you could choose more asynchronous ways of working…

... or extracting yourself all together.

> **Enough.**
>
> As a member of a network group that met each Wednesday morning at 7am, I found I felt ill after the meetings. There was something else going on there. And I was just being nice showing up and attending. I was getting more and more involved in their business and being sucked into the culture and the behaviour of the business. Vampires everywhere!
>
> The sessions were repetitive, simplistic, and at a level of knowledge that was already familiar to me. It was low/no value for me.
>
> Enough.
>
> I stopped. I pulled the pin, unplugged and sent a message saying, 'I won't be attending any more of the network sessions. They're not delivering enough value and insight for me.'
>
> A great reference right now would be the book 'Disease to Please' by Harriet B Braiker PhD. And the brilliant people-pleasing memes, tips and insights from Hailey Magee on Instagram at @haileypaigemagee.
>
> Both authors identify and name the people pleasing that many of us do. This behaviour only entangles us further and deeper, involving us more. We get sucked into more and more work ... and much of it is sync work.
>
> *Can you join this meeting?*
>
> *Can we have a quick chat?*

Are you available to get the briefing and more context?

When can we connect on this?

When are you free to meet?

But when you can step away from something sync, do it, go for it. Get the heck out. Focus on the stuff that truly matters and is more valuable and impactful.

You'll have greater flexibility of when and how you work, and it will help you achieve better outcomes in your business, team or organisation, with a lot less frustration.

Work is continuing to change. And so must we.

Instead of defaulting to 'accept' a meeting invite (synchronous work), what if you worked in another way (asynchronous work)?

An evolution of language

I think there's a new and evolving language we'll be working with.

Think of the options.

- Async work now
- Async work later
- Sync work now
- Sync work later.

It's not unlike the Eisenhower Matrix/Covey Matrix of urgent and important work, but for me, it shortcuts the language even further.

I need only think is this work for now or later?

If it's now - is it sync or async... or both?

If it's later - is it sync or async ... or both?

When we're engaging and communicating with people regarding work, perhaps we could indicate if we consider it to be work that is:

- For sync attendance.
- For sync contribution.
- For async attention.
- For async contribution.

If it's for your attention, it could be a read or watch or make note of. If it's for contribution, there are options to contribute async or sync like shared documents or visual collaboration boards. You might include a link to the options for async attention and contribution in your communication. And if it's for attendance, make it a good one!

> → **Sync Async Tip: Even if you want people to attend a sync event, we must include more ways for people to participate, contribute and be part of it without being live, there, now.**

I hope our language evolves to be able to say, 'let's sync on this' or 'I'll start async on this and then let's sync next week.'

Rather than sounding clichéd or jargonistic, I hope it becomes a sign of when things are sync and async and how we'll handle the transition between them.

> *Jude, could you and the team progress this async and then let's meet again next Tuesday.*
>
> Or
>
> *I'll start on it, async, and send through the first draft to you for your thoughts.*
>
> Or
>
> *Let me async first and I'll gather some ideas; then send out the link so the team can add to it async. We probably won't need to meet again at all.*

> Or
>
> *I'll send you a link to vote on the decision async. For queries, uncertainties or things we've missed, add to the 'and another thing' document at this link you include in your message.*

And so, it goes on, with many more async opportunities rather than defaulting to sync.

PART 3

SKILLS, TOOLS & TECHNIQUES

Lynne Cazaly

Skills for Sync Async

There is a matrix of skills for effective working in sync and async situations.

These are not the tools or technology or apps; more on that soon. But these are skills, behaviours, things that humans can think and do to make working sync async more effective, more impactful.

It's not exhaustive; it's a start.

The three main segments of skill, building from the bottom up, are:

- Information
- Range
- Progress.

PROGRESS	SPEED UP (faster)	SLOW DOWN (slower)	REPLAY (repeat)
RANGE	BROADCAST (wide)	NARROWCAST (niche)	RECAST (later)
INFORMATION	SUMMARY (facts)	SYNTHESIS (next)	SENSE MAKING (depth)

www.lynnecazaly.com

INFORMATION

When you're dealing with information in sync async work, you can use these skills to manoeuvre among and wrangle with that information.

SUMMARY

(That's summary as a skill, not a summary of what you're reading here.)

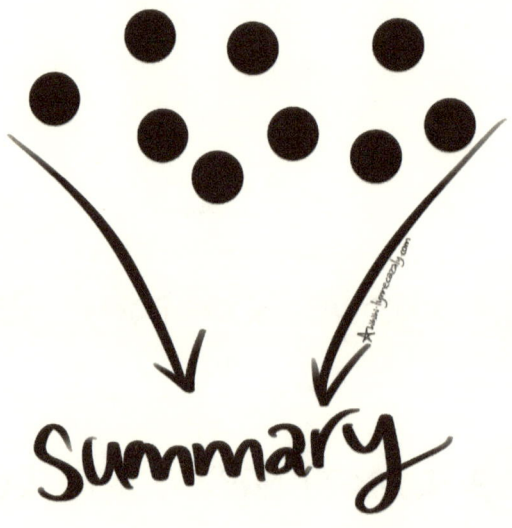

We see a summary as short explanation of a movie or series we're considering watching. These are tough to write! They don't come easily for many people, and we may only write about the first thing that happens but not link through to what else happened in an event, piece of work or a meeting.

We either cut things too short or we waffle. We're not so good at a summary on demand.

A summary also has some marketing or promotion about it. Imagine a synopsis that read: 'A boring two-hour meeting where SD rambled on about their spreadsheet and PowerPoint presentation and at the end asked, 'any questions?' '

It's feasible though isn't it!? But if instead the summary said: 'SD update on the scope of topics to be funded in the 2024/25 financial year for XYZ project phase 1.' That's potentially more helpful.

Many people love to talk and tell stories. And when we ask, 'what happened?' they may start at the beginning of the story and tell us the whole thing.

Tune in to them and you can tell when people just want to know what the outcome was. They shorten their responses: 'Yep. Yep. Yep.' is a classic response. Avoid the fluff, waffle and details.

Answer things like:

- Is everything OK?
- Did the project get funded?
- Was the timeline accepted?
- Did the client make any changes?

Cut to the chase and give the game away. It's like giving away the punchline of the joke or story at the start. And as journalists are told, 'don't bury the lead'; don't hide the bright gem or biggest point down down deep in the news article. Get it out straight away.

> *Success. The project got funded. They had three questions and Alex's team is going to respond to those. We will meet again in two weeks. BTW, Tim had a haircut! And Jem has a new cat. There's your summary.*

Is preferred to:

> *Well Deb started the meeting but then she lost connection so Tim had a haircut and the meeting when on a bit, I missed it for a while and wasn't sure what they were talking about, something to do with the project scope session, and then they said April 18, that was the key date for... can't remember sorry if it was Phase 1 or Phase 1.5 and then a few other people spoke and that was kind of it. Sorry.*

It may be the reality of your experience because you know, many meetings don't work so well, and we pay continuous partial attention, but the skill of capturing or crafting a summary will help you track the key points in the meeting so it's worthy of sharing.

Check out movies and TV series or books for brilliant examples that are close at hand.

Here's a synopsis for Top Gun the original film from a quick Google search:

> "The Top Gun Naval Fighter Weapons School is where the best of the best train to refine their elite flying skills. When hotshot fighter pilot Maverick (Tom Cruise) is sent to the school, his reckless attitude and cocky demeanour put him at odds with the other pilots, especially the cool and collected Iceman (Val Kilmer). But Maverick isn't only competing to be the top fighter pilot, he's also fighting for the attention of his beautiful flight instructor, Charlotte Blackwood (Kelly McGillis)."

Here's one for the Shondaland Netflix Bridgeton series one …

> "Bridgerton follows Daphne Bridgerton, the eldest daughter of the powerful Bridgerton family as she makes her debut onto Regency London's competitive marriage market. Hoping to follow in her parents' footsteps and find a match sparked by true love, Daphne's prospects initially seem to be unrivalled. But as her older brother begins to rule out her potential suitors, the high society scandal sheet written by the mysterious Lady Whistledown casts aspersions on Daphne. Enter the highly desirable and rebellious Duke of Hastings, committed bachelor and the catch of the season for the debutantes' mamas. Despite proclaiming that they want nothing the other has to offer, their attraction is undeniable and sparks

> *fly as they find themselves engaged in an increasing battle of wits while navigating society's expectations for their future."*

Dear Reader, if you've watched Bridgerton, you'd recognise the story here and recall the deeper details. If you haven't watched it there's plenty here to give context, scope and the opportunity to enquire or probe further. And oh my… series two, wooh!

After writing media releases in a PR job, I held some years ago, I used to love clicking on the button Microsoft Word USED TO HAVE (angry about this!) to auto-summarise. It's gone now and I'm sad and angry about that. But I'd use that brief summary as a tool to pitch the story to media or to brief the CEO before she signed off on it.

It might be gone from Word but there are plenty of specific applications and programs that will do it for you. Paste your text in and while it won't be perfect, it will be a great start at an artificially intelligent summary. Search Google for 'auto summary apps' or 'text summarising tool'.

The thing is, if you're the designated representative who is attending a sync meeting while your colleagues are working async, when they ask you 'what happened in the meeting?', you'd better be able to answer beyond 'not much'! Even if not much happened in the meeting, you can still provide a summary and be helpful and responsible to your colleagues.

Summarise as you go. I'll often take quick typed notes - not court reporter level transcription but quick summary notes as it happens. Don't try and catch up later.

If in doubt, capture three of the main key points. Three is a freakin' magic number. It's more than enough to get started and can show the scope or scale of something. You know, beginning, middle, end. Knife fork spoon. Rain hail shine. We're surrounded by the 'Rule of Threes' everywhere, so three dot points are magic under a heading.

You could also use three-word genres like streaming services do: Quirky. Romance. Adventure. or Sci Fi. Escape. War.

From my time working in the music industry, I remember how we loved to use the phrase 'file between' so you can give people an idea of the style, type or genre of music you're about to play or recommend… and where you'd find it in a music library. You'd might know what 'filed between The Go-Gos and Beyonce' would sound like. Or you might not.

Broadcasters trying to entice you to watch something new sell it to you with descriptions like 'if you liked Game of Thrones then you might like House of the Dragon'.

Imagine this technique at use at work:

If you didn't like Jamie's meeting about the legislation in March, this won't be for you.

Or

Worth watching the replay. The new product features, latest customer data and marketing campaign details are all there. The best bits start at time stamp 17:06.

As I walked past my local primary school, along the fence line this week, the door was open to one of the classrooms. Ventilation, right? I could hear the teacher saying to the room as they walked among the students, 'What are the key points? What is your summary of the story? If someone walked into class now and hadn't read the story, what would you tell them? If you only had one minute, what would you tell them it was about? Let's write that down now… Go!'

Summaries are an important and fundamental part of how we think, work, communicate and share information. No wonder they're learning it at school. Get summaries working for you as you sync async.

SYNTHESIS

Now, synthesis, this is a different skill. It's taking a synopsis or a summary and adding more. It's connecting more content and thinking. It could be adding your opinions, insights and perspectives.

For example, to synthesize a series of meetings could be to show how the content advanced or moved on from one meeting or workshop to the next. And then, adding in some thoughts about what could be next, what else it's about, what the bigger thinking is or what else you think is required.

A client of mine is hosting a series of customer conversations and while some people think that every workshop will be the same, they won't be. You could summarise the content and outcomes, yes, but then you could synthesize things to take them further.

You could suggest or help make progress by:
- showing how the thinking and themes in the conversations changed over time
- identifying suggested next steps
- providing some topics that could warrant further investigation
- connecting to global or local trends.

With synthesis as a skill for sync async work, you consider bringing in other sources, examples, ideas, perspectives and opinions.

- You could share data from an industry leading business.
- Or weave in the thinking from some recent research on the topic.
- Share and connect the work done by other parts of the organisation.
- Tie in the earlier or previous work completed.
- Visualise the bigger picture or map that this work could be part of.

The key is to not just summarise something but to truly help **advance** the work and to do that, you need to bring in other content, sources or ideas.

It's such a helpful skill in sync async work because it's focused on what's happened AND what's next. You can't help but make great progress when you're considering the next steps.

SENSEMAKING

Read and learn more about sensemaking in my book 'Making Sense: A Handbook for the Future of Work'.

The Institute for the Future quoted sensemaking as one of the top skills we'd need in the changing world of work.

Sensemaking is trying to determine what is going on and what we need to do about it… even when we are uncertain about what's going on! It's working out what the deeper meaning of something is. It can involve a range of different tools, techniques, frameworks and methodologies. From questions, listening and sketching, to data collection, visual mapping and model creation. The visual side of sensemaking is one of my preferences. And one of the reasons why, is that it helps us create an artefact of actuality!

We can make sense throughout everyday activities by

having conversations, sharing stories, asking questions, writing, thinking, reflecting, observing and researching. Notice that many of these are active behaviours. Sensemaking is often referred to as an 'emergent' activity; that is, some of the things we discover or find out may not be known until we start talking, working, or making sense!

While we might make sense a little 'automatically' when problem solving or trying to work out what has happened, we can also apply our skills of sensemaking in deliberate and measured ways.

Summaries, synthesis and sensemaking. Let's imagine two or three of these tools working together.

What if you did a summary *and* some synthesizing? What a beautiful tool or artifact for people who are working asynchronously! Then bring the third technique of sensemaking in and that would lift the knowledge, insight and information to a whole new level that becomes even more useful and practical for a team.

You can label the information you're creating, sharing or documenting with these skills so people know what they're getting from you.

Here's an example:

> *Hi Dom, here's a <u>summary</u> from the Tuesday meeting with product team. And you'll also find my thoughts and <u>synthesis</u> on what we could do for our next steps. A map was created in the meeting to <u>make sense</u> of the customer feedback*

and I think it's a useful collection of the latest information on the product plan.

Here's the thing about async: it's not just people working alone, independently in the dark. When you apply the skills of summaries, synthesis and sensemaking, you'll be making some great progress individually and together. You just can't help but make progress.

RANGE

If we've got more information and communication floating about in a sync async world, how on earth do we deal with it all?

The thinking here comes to how wide you want that information to go: the range. This is a vital consideration when working async.

Default behaviours have us cc-ing everyone, sending to the whole list and replying all. All all all. But that often involves more people than necessary and entangles them – and us – deeper.

Consider the different breadths and depths and the range of distribution. I do believe this is a skill. We need to stop and think and look at what we're working on, who's involved and who's missing. It's being **discerning**, **astute** and **considerate** all at once. It's easy to default to include everyone or we accidentally exclude someone.

Here's what I mean:

BROADCAST

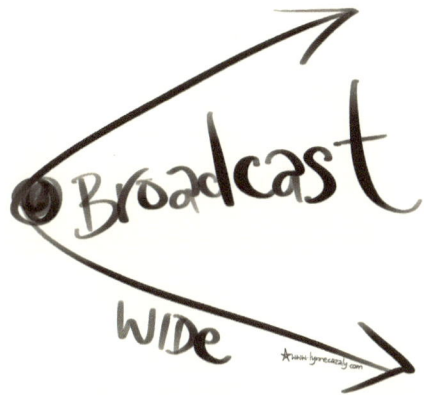

Think all of staff, or the whole team, or everyone on the project. Not everything needs to be broadcast widely but it's an option.

It's the 'all now' approach. It's like pressing a 'go live' button… a BIG RED BUTTON like the ON AIR signs that seem to shout at you at a radio or TV station.

Keep this for big announcements, important revelations and significant developments.

Some teams save these for newsletters, video updates or Monday morning or Friday afternoon podcast broadcasts. There are leaders among us who are revelling in the podcast broadcast: a short broadcast about the week just gone or the one ahead or a briefing on the ~~shit~~ stuff that's going down. They record it using the voice memo on their phone when it suits them, and it gets shared for you to listen when it suits you.

'Leadership communication through private podcasting can establish a more personal relationship between employees', says Jen Grogono in Forbes Magazine, 'especially with those workers who are remote and might already feel distant from headquarters.'

It offers inclusion and a bringing together of people. It doesn't have to be a live-in-the-moment-all-here-looking-at-each-other Town Hall gathering. A broadcast is another way.

NARROWCAST

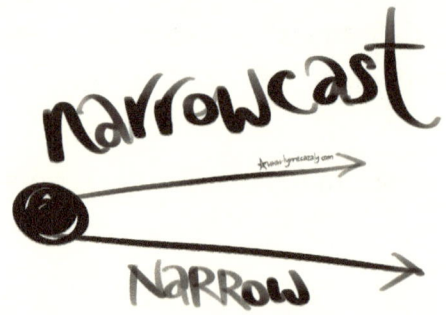

Narrow it down some and you'll have a range of information and communication with some people, not all. Think the marketing team; the team in the Bay area; recent arrivals or new starters; new to leadership roles; people of colour; women. Get it… you target some now and if there's a recording or a replay, others can watch, listen or contribute later.

Making links available to get involved if you want to, helps spread the love. It doesn't force you via a broadcast.

A technology team I work with share a video update on Wednesday morning just for the software developers. It's helping build their cohesion as a team, their capability as significant members of the project and building a team of ambassadors or advocates for the project. Not everyone is invited but the recordings aren't hidden. It's more of this transparency stuff, right?

RECAST

If you've watched a catch-up program on mainstream or free-to-air TV you've enjoyed the power of a recast. Miss it live and you can catch up later. The recast is a powerful way of helping people do the async stuff they want, flexibly when it suits them. And listening to or watching something they didn't have to attend live is mighty powerful.

Walk the dog; pave the backyard; sit with the kids at sport; drive in the car; have a coffee; do some stretches;

sit in the sun.

All these situations allow us the opportunity to multitask safely.

See, we already do Netflix async. We can be watching the same things, just not at the same time or up to the same episodes.

And yeah, but … there'll be too much to catch up on.

If you're thinking there's too much to catch up on, you could be seeing it through the eyes of a weekly schedule full of 2 – 3-hour meetings. Yes, you won't be able to get through it all live in the moment, sync.

But async?

- Watching a recording, sped up say 1.5 times? That's more doable.
- Searching the transcript for when they started talking about the stuff that's relevant to you; that's more manageable.

And yeah, but … some people won't watch it.

True. Some people won't watch it. We don't want to force people to endure dullness.

Make it:

- shorter

- audible

- readable, searchable, scannable, speedable,

repeatable, accessible

and then spend time making the work more engaging and interesting. Then they'll watch it. And tell their colleagues, friends and co-workers about it!

PROGRESS

To make better progress working sync async, remember to work at different speeds. Not everything can be achieved at the same speed. Quick messages, short meetings and brief conversations can be done at different speeds to lengthy workshops, long documents and deep conversations.

Choose difference depending on the situation.

SPEED UP

Just like we push down on the car accelerator when we have open road or structured freeways and motorways to travel more safely in, so we can with sync async work.

When work is flowing, we can often pick up the pace and accelerate. It's not that everything is too slow – although many presentations are – but we can often tolerate a quicker pace of listening, following along and understanding information. Often. Not always.

So, do a speed check.

Use the buttons on online meeting platforms like Zoom that indicate 'speed up' or 'slow down'. Ask people to make use of them throughout the session or sync work. And in async work, ask people if they're ready for the next step or to move on to the next piece of work. Check the speed with them. Is this too slow for you? Can we move along now?

Over-explaining, starting at the beginning to give an overly long context and giving unnecessary historical stories could be all speed up signals.

Keeping a steady and optimal flow of work in both sync and async is important. Momentum is great and the progress is motivating.

Just remember to up the speed ... as an option. It helps people stay interested, engaged and energised. If it's too slow… it's hypnotically slow and just not enough for our brain to do. That's when people look for distractions.

SLOW DOWN

If you've 'got a lot to get through' then you might be at risk of going too fast. As time diminishes, we tend to talk quicker and skip through content in meetings or miss important things.

You may need to slow down.

Slowing down on one thing doesn't mean the whole thing needs to be slow.

Slowing down as you get to a crunch point or delivery date with work is natural, to check details and process final approvals.

And slowing down when we're working across languages, cultures and time zones could be a must. This is where checking the pace or speed with your colleagues is generous, kind and patient.

REPLAY

A frustration can creep into us when we need to replay or revisit something. But we may need to go over something more than once. Some people need to hear or read or see things more than once to process and 'get' them.

There's nothing wrong with that. It's how we absorb and understand.

You know the 'don't take that tone with me' statement when someone is getting angry or frustrated? Watch out for it. Your frustration in having to replay something can 'leak out of us' in our voice, the words we write, our facial expressions and body language.

I'm a keen listener to air traffic control (such an #avgeek) and the air traffic controller's lack of tone when repeating information to pilots is stunning to hear. There's no 'why didn't you hear it the first time?' attitude. They repeat information three times or more if needed and correct the elements of information transmitted, minus tone or attitude. Like this:

Control Tower: Emirates 408, take taxiways Alpha Echo Juliet (AEJ) to Runway 27 left, and line up and wait'

Pilot: 'Alpha Juliet Echo (AJE) Runway 27 left, line up and wait'.

Control Tower: 'Negative. That's Alpha Echo Juliet (AEJ).'

Pilot: 'Alpha Echo Juliet'. 27 Left. Line up and wait.

The replay is given. No tone, no attitude. Just accuracy and engagement. Not louder, not slower. A replay.

Be considerate in replaying information – whether it's written, verbal, recorded or transcribed.

These are some different ways of working and it may take some time to adjust to using different modes or tools, and to taking in information in different ways. Delivering tone and attitude when repeating information – as in 'didn't you HEAR me' – isn't pleasant, kind or inclusive.

Get started and make progress with asynchronous work.

Tools for Sync Async

The main tool to use for sync async work is your brain! You can decide that this is how you're going to work.

Deliberately.

To help you in that, to engage and communicate with others, you may like to use some **tools** to take things out of sync and real time and put them in to async mode.

Consider the **role** the tool plays and how it can help you and the team work well synchronously and even better asynchronously.

For example, instead of thinking 'we need to use *Slack*', consider if you need a team messaging platform where you can share information and attach documents.

Instead of thinking 'we need to use *Loom*', think how can we make and share simple and short video updates.

Marcelo Lebre says in 'Why you should be working asynchronously in 2022' that some of the best, best practices for asynchronous communication are:

- good documentation

- written procedures

- messaging over calls

- respect for interruption-free work slots.

And what happens when these kinds of practices are adopted and followed is that the impact or disruption on work flow itself is little, but the execution the individuals and teams are able to deliver or achieve is greater.

I reckon we think it's the reverse; we think that disrupting or interrupting someone isn't a big deal and that writing things down or sending or leaving messages isn't effective. Ummm, but it is. It's the absolute reverse on both counts.

If you only focused on these four elements of asynchronous work – documentation, written procedures, messages and respect – you'd get to a pretty good place. A place where you are making more and better progress.

And what if you just focused on one of them to get started? That's a great start.

To go deeper into tools, there are several options available for every tool you can choose from.

Think of tools like:

- Emailing
- Surveys
- Voice messages
- Texting
- Meeting 1:1
- Meeting prior
- Meeting after

- Written chat
- Videos
- Conversation small group
- Conversation large group

… and onward.

I'm explaining the following tools generically: the application, software, system or program you use is up to you and dependent on the evolution of, and entrants to (and departures from) the technical world! And whether you work in an organisation that already has designated tools for async work.

Many of the tool companies themselves provide resources and blogs for how to not only make the best use of their stuff, but they publish guides, playbooks (which is a cooler name than 'guide') and tip sheets on how to work well with the tool. Their content creating marketing teams are working double time. Hopefully, async.

Anyway… check the tech. Who are they and what are they about? If their product is for a specific aspect of sync or async work, that will probably be their push. Hey, we're all biased!

And Google it; you'll find a bunch of the latest applications, services, software and programs there for the searching. There are plenty of articles reviewing different choices and videos where reviewers have shared their experiences and tips. Search for things like 'the 10 best messaging platforms for work' or 'the best shared documents apps' or try 'best apps for summaries' or 'best tools for video'. Get it? That way you'll get to see the range of what's out there.

Let's go...

- **Group documents/shared documents**

I was a delegate in an online conference recently and one of the presenters broke us into breakout rooms in Zoom - no need to groan. They shared a document link with us all and we all opened that document, viewing it online. In our groups of three people, we had specific pages allocated in the document with topics we were listing problems and generating ideas for. After a 15-minute breakout session, BOOM, ka-BOOM the document was FULL. All of the sections full and all of the topics had contributions under them. We all downloaded the document as our mega-takeaway of collated notes from the 15-minute session. 15 easy minutes of effort from about 35 people. Epic work.

No days, weeks, months collecting drips of content nor excruciating 'let's brainstorm this' meetings. Everyone contributing. Now this is active participation. Synchronous. But you know what, we have the link, the document is still there, and IT'S BEEN ADDED TO! After the event, people thought of more things to add AND they had somewhere to put them. Awesome resource. Easily done. Asynchronously updated. And continuously available for ideas as they grow over time.

- **Task Boards**

Seeing what work is currently in progress across a team or project and what's coming up is a highly effective way of working.

Based on the popular lean manufacturing process, Kanban, putting visual boards online or in real life on a wall can be quite easily shared and they help a team or group manage their workflow. Current popular applications like Trello, Monday, LeanKit help us see what we're working on and the process and progress we're making. I use a Kanban board for my daily work as well as for bigger projects… like writing this book! I love these tools for async. Love. Love. Love.

- **Videos and Screen Capture**

If you wanted to record a video or capture the work or comments from your screen, you could use any number of video applications to produce, shoot, edit, upload, screen share, transcribe, post, share, subtitle. It's less about the app you use; more that you chose to communicate, capture and work with video. The moving image with sound, music, colour, light, brightness, text and type is captivating for sure.

From working in the film industry at the Open Channel Co-operative some years ago, and being on the board of management there, I've seen the skills and opportunities for film making become so levelled, accessible and fantastic! No longer do we need to enrol in a lengthy course to learn the skills or book out a fancy studio to make our production. There is much learning we can do for ourselves through experimentation.

> *This tweet from Jeffrey Brady:*
>
> *If you don't know about Loom, you should check it out. I used it to provide feedback recordings to my students on their writing assignments. It allowed me to record the screen showing their essay as I provided them verbal feedback of highlighted sections I wanted them to revise. I found it much easier than attempting to type all of my comments.*

Check out the work of colleagues Mo McCrae, Julian Mather, Rebecca Saunders, and Cam Fink. They are all great proponents and supporters of the use of video and help you build the skills, get over your fears and make best use of the simplest tools possible to deliver the best outcomes. Five stars for all of them!

And are you thinking short video? Why does it have to be short? Short is good for viewing, cut through and engagement, sure. But long is great for that detailed coverage of content that can be shared, re-watched, paused, sped up, broken down and re-watched.

I've been watching longer videos of 60-90 minutes on narcissistic behaviour. I've learned so much about the narc's manipulation tactics, lies, sneaky behaviours and tragic childhoods. I speed the videos up at 1.5 - 2 x the normal viewing speed. I still absorb the content, in quick time. I'm not studying for an exam or aiming to pass a psychological entrance test. It's personal learning and awareness and ... wow, now I'm aware at about 1/3 of the time of watching them in real time simply by increasing the playback speed. It's also made me realise that all of those meetings, those sync 'it's about me' sessions could be perpetuated and continued by people with narcissistic tendencies. All the more reason to offer and participate with an async solution. It's a saviour and a self-protector from the narc-BS.

- **Audio recordings and messages**

The podcast craze hasn't grown because of good marketing. It's that a lot of us prefer to listen and hear. That may not be you though and that's ok. You might like to talk a lot. In that case, an audio recording could be great for others to listen to. Get it? It may not be your preference to listen, but you might like to talk.

I worked in radio broadcasting for years and the psychology and production power of audio alone are so captivating. Sound effects, intimacy, that direct 1:1 communication. It was always believed that you had a captive audience when a listener was driving in their car with the radio on or in that solitary world of wearing headphones. It's the personal and private space of the interior of your car, or the intimacy of headphones delivering audio content directly to you that works so well.

Don't ever discount audio. It's so much more powerful than we realise.

I sent an audio message to my colleague and friend Tanya. I was going to send a text-based message. But then saw the microphone icon and recorded a 'Hi Tanya, thought I'd speak you a message today…' message. She remarked on how personal it was, that she was able to re-listen to it and pause to pick up the details. And she's kept it so she can revisit the information if required. It prompted her to start using audio messages herself because of how it worked for her and impacted her.

- **Texts and SMS**

These are frequently known as the immediate message or the cut through mode of communicating with someone. When they've got messaging silenced on their work apps or aren't checking email for another few hours, a text message could be the ultimate async tool.

You send it when it suits you.

They read it when it suits them.

This could include social media messages that you receive within the platform or app.

But given many of us can't look away from our devices, we often see a text message come through or we see the notification bell or symbol alerting us to one being there.

Messages though… you can forward them, copy and paste, reply, screenshot them for use in other applications, presentations, marketing or documentation.

- **Email**

Email could be good again

Well… for non-urgent things anyway!

Instead of being a black hole and a block in your workday, communication by email can start to be useful again when we're working more async. Async starts to free up your mind and your time. Therefore, some of the communication channels we might have previously rolled our eyes at because we 'just didn't have time' or bandwidth to read, review or scan, start to become pivotal tools for async.

Instead of worrying about the number of emails in your inbox, you will have time (if you don't go to that meeting today), to scan through your email inbox and identify the tasks that require your:

- synchronous attendance, or
- asynchronous attention.

That's it. These are really the only two things to look at and sort or prioritise for.

Then ask: What's the next step?

- **Direct messages**

The DM – sent via social platforms or during an online call on a meeting platform. We can send direct communications with people while we are in sync situations, but we can also direct message people on a whole range of platforms: social media, workflow tools, or work and project management apps.

It's an example of the Range that I covered earlier, being really narrowed down. Giving people direct 'for your information', or 'heads up' messages can be truly helpful.

- **Visual Canvas/Collaboration**

The rise of online visual platforms, visual noticeboards and virtual whiteboards has grown in popularity over recent years. And their features, templates and capabilities are growing too!

Search 'best online whiteboards for collaboration' or similar and you'll see there are plenty to choose from and a variety of pricing plans from free to plenty.

One of the big features of virtual collaboration providers like Mural or Miro is their range of templates for different types of meetings and consultations. You don't ever have to start with a blank page if you don't want to. Click on a template and you're away, as it automatically sets out columns, titles, spaces and topics for you and your colleagues to collaborate and contribute.

Not only are they great for async work – that is, add your contributions before or after a meeting or conversation – but they're great for sync meetings and conversations. Earlier when I mentioned the preferrable active and valuable benefits of sync versus those passive wasteful situations … it can be these types of visual tools that keep people thinking, active, contributing and engaged.

And then you've got yourself an artefact of actuality! They're a win-win-win for me.

- **Comments and annotations**

Think of where you want to make your mark or leave your comments and opinions.

When we share documentation, and we've been asked to comment, we can reply with an email and put comments in there or add our comments and annotations on the pages of the document. Many shared documents and PDFs etc have this available as an option. It's a great way to edit a document as you can have people's comments and thoughts right there in the document where you're working. And you can 'resolve' or delete comments as they're worked on or completed. Books are commonly edited like this and it's so good to hear from an editor with a comment like, 'What's this? Need more description here' or 'Source for this quote?' or 'Love this; consider dedicating a section or more content for this.'

This is a wonderfully powerful way to contribute async and I think we overlook it. The default could be that in sync work we're expected to give our comments as the droning presentation is being delivered. This can allow you to scan a deck in your own time and add what you think in that 'clear air' I mentioned earlier in Part 2.

- **Dot points**

Dot points are the cousin or sibling to summaries. They drag out focus from a waffly paragraph. They help us:

- focus our attention
- vary our reading rhythm, shifting us out of a kind of hypnosis, and
- show breadth or dimension to the information.

But don't use too many in a list. After a few dot points we tend to doze off. But a few, say, 3 – 5 is just fine.

- **Chat**

My business manager, Myra and I will often chat via the project management software we use to manage tasks and work. It works across our phones and laptops and desktops and it keeps like work or relevant conversations within the application we use for work. We don't tend to talk holidays and personal lives in that project management chat. We tend to save that for email exchanges.

Whatsapp groups have become so popular in recent years and help narrow both your **information** and **range**.

- **Playback Speed, Tags and Chapters**

Recordings of a meeting with hashtags listed or chapters

marked give us the ability to rapidly determine relevance. We can then adjust the playback speed to skip fast forward or go back and rewind a section. Equally we can cut to the chase and get to the bits that really matter to us and skip the rest.

I reckon this is the biggest thing about sync meetings that we can't do. We can't fast forward people in real life. We might try with clichéd phrases like, 'we've got to move on' or 'we're running out of time, so I'll just do this quickly'. We KNOW we're dragging things out and hearing this is to me, a big sign that an async moment has been missed.

Hashtags or chapters marked on recordings mean we can get what we need … and then get out.

And when someone asks, 'will there be a recording?' they're crying out for an async opportunity. Give it to them.

- **Transcripts**

I LOVE me a transcript of a recording of an online meeting. Yes, the spoken word translation to text may not be 100% accurate but you get the gist.

We can scan or keyword search for our areas of interest, project key words, names, issues or products.

A client team I work with searches chat files from meeting recordings and looks for their department name, their projects and team member's names so they're able to see when they're being talked about. Oh, in a nice way of course… or in a way that needs resolving.

'Hey, Pat, I noticed you mentioned the CS team in the huddle this morning and planning for the Phase 3 launch. Would you like more information? Do you have specific questions? (Note the closed questions for yes/no answer. And also note, there's no invite to sync, 'would you like a quick chat?') Clarify the need first before drowning in 'quick chats'.

- **Subtitles**

For accessibility, readability, translation and comprehension, subtitles are rocking our world. Increasingly people are using them while watching TV and streaming services, videos and recordings.

They can help with understanding, help us catch things we missed or were muffled, and can be easier on our cognitive processing than watching someone's mouth move and listening to what they say.

As we speed up replays, captions can help us zip through content if we're fast readers. And they absolutely help those whose primary languages may not be the ones being spoken in the meeting or for people with disabilities who value reading or using text to speech or text to audio features.

- **Visualisation**

Visualisation of the work - using task or shared boards like Kanban from lean manufacturing mentioned earlier -

gives you opportunities for both seeing what's going on and collaborating on it. But it could be any type of visual tool and visualised information.

Many teams use this type of work as their 'single source of truth', rather than having information scattered among different documents, diaries, emails and in chat messages.

If you know me or have read or seen any of my 'stuff' you'll know that visuals feature heavily. The advantages and benefits are many, but visual notes, graphic recordings and visual captures not only serve as a documented reminder about key themes or decisions; they also serve as a visual anchor for our storage and recollection skills.

We know how well a photograph can bring back a flood of memories about how we were feeling, other things that happened, what we had for lunch, what we were wearing, who said what. The same occurs with visual notes. They anchor incredible detail in our brain and allow for great recall.

Read more and build your skills with visuals in my books:

- *Visual Mojo: How to Capture Thinking, Convey Information and Collaborate Using Visuals.*
- *Making Sense: A Handbook for the Future of Work.*

Added to the benefits of externalising information, getting it out of our heads and somewhere that we can share and look at, we help empty our brain.

That leaves us room to problem solve, think and do more detailed mental work and means we don't feel like a zombie at the end of a day of synchronous and passive meetings.

Read more in my book *'Argh! Too much information, not enough brain: A Practical Guide to Outsmarting Overwhelm'*.

And think beyond words too. Use icons, photography, sketches, lines, shapes …

- **Knowledge management and encloypedias**

Wikipedias, knowledge management and retrieval systems, are the places to go to read about the history, events, versions, and iterations of work. Yes, it can take a lot to create and keep them up to date, but this is part of becoming a more sync async team or business. Documentation many people can access is a big part of taking the pressure off sync meetings.

For example, if I've taken notes in a meeting, I can upload them or share them in an encyclopaedia about the project or the phase of the project, and add the dates of the meeting, and the topics covered can be tagged.

Documentation is a key part of transparency and progress in the modern workplace. If people can access the information they need, they won't need to 'have a quick chat' that can take 90 minutes and spawn 6 other meetings because 'no one seems to know what's going on so let's get everyone in the same room and work out what's going on'. Oh no!

Yes, there are more tools for sure. It's not an exhaustive list so it will be fascinating to see what other tools arrive into the marketplace as our work evolves and clever start-ups and developers work out what we might need. This space will keep on changing.

Techniques for Sync Async

Beyond skills and tools for sync async, I believe there are a few key techniques you can use as needed:

Stop sync in a second

If you've started something synchronously and it's not working or you defaulted to sync without considering async, it's not too late. You can make a switch.

Right away. Immediately.

Say 'oops on second thought… this could have been set up as async. Let's end this sync situation stat and I will get your input asynchronously.'

Then work out your async plan for making the work happen that you were going to do in that passive sync thing.

Push back on the invite

This could be a big one folks. It's about how to say 'no', 'not now' or 'not ever' to some of the meeting requests, quick chats and invites you receive … or the ones that seem to magically appear in your schedule! How did it get there??

It's also about what to do when people want 'a quick chat' or want to 'grab you for a couple of minutes'. What's with all the grabbing?

When people want to get started with async work, and

don't want to have to wait until their team or organisation has a formalised strategy about it, here's what I suggest they do first.

Tackle the meetings you're invited to.

If 12 people are invited and 6 people ask these questions, it puts the pressure back on the convener to do better when sync work is requested or expected.

The action is to push back on the meeting to create a way to contribute async and to get some more time in your week.

The phrase 'push back' is one of those clichés or jargon terms that drives half of us bonkers and validates the other half of us who use the term, even if only in our own mind.

The idea of pushing back is about resistance to something … or as I prefer, deploying the **clarify and specify** technique.

The way I see it, there are two parts to the technique. It's not just deleting or declining the invite.

There is the **clarify** part and then the **specify** part.

Here's how it can work:
- Let's say you've got six invitations in your diary for meetings. Pick a meeting you'd rather not attend. It might be because it:

- is at an inconvenient time,
- doesn't seem fully relevant to your work,
- is clashing with something important, you know, lunch
- might not be described clearly enough
- might be assumed you'll just be there with no indication of why
- gets to gobble up two hours of your already busy day, or
- it's a regular meeting and it's never been that valuable.

- Contact the convener, host or organiser of that meeting to **clarify.**

- Ask a big wide and open **clarifying** question like:

'Hey Damien, Why am I invited to this meeting? Why am I needed there?' (Hello coaches who are triggered by 'why' questions. Change it to a 'What is the reason I'm invited to this meeting? What do you need me there for?)

If the response makes good sense to you, then good-o, get along to the meeting and pick another one in your schedule. But if a response comes back and you're still not sure why you're supposed to be there, use the **specify** part of the technique:

- *'Thanks Damien. What **specifically** do you need me to do at this meeting?'*

Damien might say it's because you're part of the Big Blah project. So, ask again: *'And what specifically will be happening at the meeting that requires my attendance?'*

If the response makes good sense to you, then good-o, get along to the meeting and pick another one in your schedule. See the pattern here?

If it doesn't make sense, you can go again and ask.

Now we're up to question three. But I tell you, it's worth the effort. If it takes you three emails of about 90 seconds work each to understand why you need to be there and what you have to do, it's way better than just baaaa sheeping yourself along and following everyone else to a meeting that's going to suck two hours, and the joy and life out of you. It could be a **passive** and **wasteful** experience.

- Ask Damien a neat, closed question, needing yes or no answers:

'Do you need me to:

- Report on something Y/N
- Be informed about something Y/N
- Be included in the discussion Y/N'

Depending on their response, if you're needed to do something **active** and **valuable**, like report on something, or contribute or decide, then it's up to you to either attend, or just attend for the portion of the meeting where you're needed.

For example:

'Ok, thanks Damien. This is helpful. I'll attend for presenting the report only; could you let me know approximately what time that is scheduled, and I'll join the meeting a little before that time and depart after my presentation.'

OR

'Ok, thanks Damien. I can't attend the meeting, but I will contribute my thoughts for the discussion topic prior to the meeting if you send me details about what you're wanting input on. And if there is an information pack to review or a discussion to catch up on, I'll check the recording, read the pack over the next week or speak with Aja to get a report on the meeting.'

Seriously. This. You can do it. These are important things. It's assertive behaviour and it is something that allows you greater choice to work in ways that suit you and help you deliver great value to the organisation you agreed to work for.

Many meetings suck so badly because the opportunities for async aren't there. They're just never presented or made obvious by the meeting host or convener. But you can make async opportunities happen. You do this by using the **clarify** and **specify** questions…. And you're kind of specifying what you're going to do, how you'll contribute.

Of course, as mentioned earlier, some sync things are **passive** but they're **valuable** too. The new CEO is delivering an insight to the quarter's results and plans for the next quarter's strategy; the Procurement Manager is summarising the new legislative requirements for purchasing supplies; the Catering Team Leader is revealing the new Autumn menu… haha, you get it though, right? It's fairly passive (here, sit and listen to this, watch the slides, don't say anything, don't speak, don't think) and it could well be a total waste, or it could have some value.

Stay alert to meeting requests and push back soon after you receive them, not 15 minutes before the meeting or even on the day of the meeting. That's not fair on the convener. If you push back soon after you receive the invitation, with a **clarify** request, then the convener has the opportunity to reframe or reissue the invite or hopefully, cancel the meeting realising the work can be done asynchronously. This can happen when when you make suggestions about how you'll contribute asynchronously. The meeting convener might think,

'Hey, that's a great idea. I'll get everyone to do that and won't need a meeting.'

Here are a few push back takeaways:

Remember the direct actions you can take to rid your schedule of meetings are:

1. Pushing back and not attending some meetings, but that doesn't mean not contributing, because you will still contribute your suggestions and input, but you choose to do it in an asynchronous way.

2. Asking people why you are required at a sync event and letting them tell you why. Instead of assuming that they know why you need to be there, let them tell you why you need to be there and what is expected of you. So much unspoken communication happens where assumptions are made and people are invited to meetings that are unnecessary.

3. Try it. Try a full day of asynchronous work. Try a week of asynchronous work. And yes, you may well miss interacting with people. It might also reveal what apps or tools you could use that would help you stay across, connected and in the flow of things without it being all sync.

Get started on it

Another powerful technique for async work is called 'getting started'. Ok, I'm being a little cheeky here, but that's what you do… you get started on a task and you don't wait until a certain person is available or back from leave or out of a meeting. Send through your initial thinking or prepare some notes or a document or a map or a model or a visual framework of your thoughts.

Don't wait for a busy person; get started!

Trust your expertise

You're employed or a business owner/consultant because you know stuff. Lots of it. Now is a great time to apply this knowledge.

Many people default to a passive position, waiting to be told what to do next. It could be that we genuinely don't know what to do next and need the guidance, or perhaps we've fallen into a habit of defaulting to ask others. Maybe we're fearful that if we take too much initiative, we might mess up or make mistakes.

But please get started and use your initiative.

Default to Action

Keep thinking 'How do I move to the next step? What is the next action? Is it my step?'

And consider:
Am I holding on, holding up or handing off?

As many teams and leaders who are increasingly working in this way, they associate async with action, taking action. As Marcelo Lebre says in the Remote.com article, 'it's not about procedure, it's about attitude'.

Ask for specific feedback

When asking for feedback, be helpful and let people know what **specific** feedback you're after. Let them know what section or part or piece you want their input on.

Here's one I received recently:

'Hey Lynne, here's a draft of my whitepaper. I'd love your feedback.'

Wow, that's such a wide scope to give feedback on. I wonder if they want feedback on: writing style, design, argument, sales pitch, length, comprehension, accessibility, uniqueness. I mean the list is endless! Give people some parameters so they can accelerate their input and give you the stuff you truly need. Like this:

'Hey Lynne, here's a draft of my whitepaper. I'd love your feedback on the look of it and whether it would suit a corporate market. And I'd be interested if you see anything missing from the sales section on page 12. Apart from that, I think I'm good.'

Get started on it.

Use your initiative and pick up a task to work on.

Async
lets people
work at their
speed,
in their way
and
in their
sequence.

Taking Action

A STRATEGY for more async

Here are some other resources and tools to help you out. If your team or organisation is keen to develop a strategy for adopting more async work, try these steps:

1. **WASTE: Calculate the passivity.** Get real and aware to how inefficient sync is for you. Tally up times, hours, dates, people and really see the numbers for what they are.

2. **REDIRECT: Allocate it to activity.** Move your important tasks to the spaces where sync work used to be.

3. **PRODUCTIVITY: Focus for clarity**. Use uninterrupted blocks of time to get the things done that matter.

4. **LEVERAGE: Meet with brevity**. Make the most of the times you are in sync and together with other humans. Keep gatherings brief and valuable and if they wane, switch to async.

5. **SAFETY: Collaborate with inclusivity**. Use a mix of sync async to make better progress and include everyone across the team or organisation. You'll be more likely to meet people's needs and help them work in ways that suit them.

Taking Action
A STORY for more async

Friend, colleague and change leadership experts, Josie Iuliano, shared some successes she's experiencing by adopting more async work.

She says:

'I've experimented with a few tasks like retrospectives, strategy feedback, program shaping and so on.

In the Retrospective for example, I've started by reducing our sync time from 55 minutes down to 30 minutes.

I send out a link to an online Mural/visual collaboration board a week prior so everyone can go online and go into the board. This gives people an opportunity to start putting in their thoughts at a time that suits them in the lead up to the sync meeting. It could be when they have a spare 5-10 minutes or at a scheduled time that suits them.

What I've noticed is there's more feedback and participation than when we did this only sync.

I'm noticing that:

- people aren't put on the spot, and they have more time to think or input at a time that's more suitable for them. Some people might be better in the morning than afternoon.
- there's more honesty because no one is watching

them as they put in their feedback, so this is encouraging psychological safety in the team.

- there is more open discussion and more people are participating due to it being a safer and more collaborative situation.
- they have a second opportunity to put further feedback into the visual collaboration or elaborate on their thoughts during the sync session.

Because of these great results, we're now getting deeper on some of the systemic issues that exist. Plus, we're solving those silent problems that everyone thinks about, and no one typically says out loud.'

It's so great to read and hear real examples of the changes people are making and the benefits they're experiencing.

Now, how about you?

→ Using Josie's story and example, how could you apply some action towards working in more async ways? Where could you start?

Taking Action
A MAP for more async

Here's how working sync async could look; it's a little like a map or a group of roads coming together and apart.

If you get together to sync and then never allow people to work independently or asynchronously, you have them glued to an everyone-always-same-time thread.

Sadly, plenty of workshops and meetings bring plenty of people together for a big gathering and then... taper off, drift away and fade off into the distance. Nothing happens after the event; nothing seems to work too well. It looks like this...

Lynne Cazaly

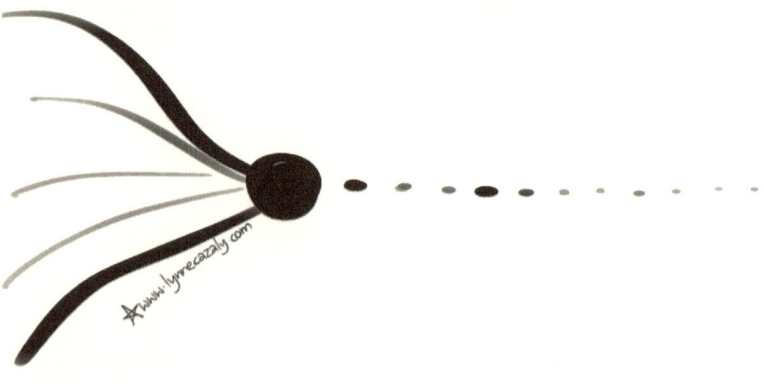

If you come together sync and then never worked sync again, that first time was it … it could look like this. You may drift apart so it's worth upping your async game.

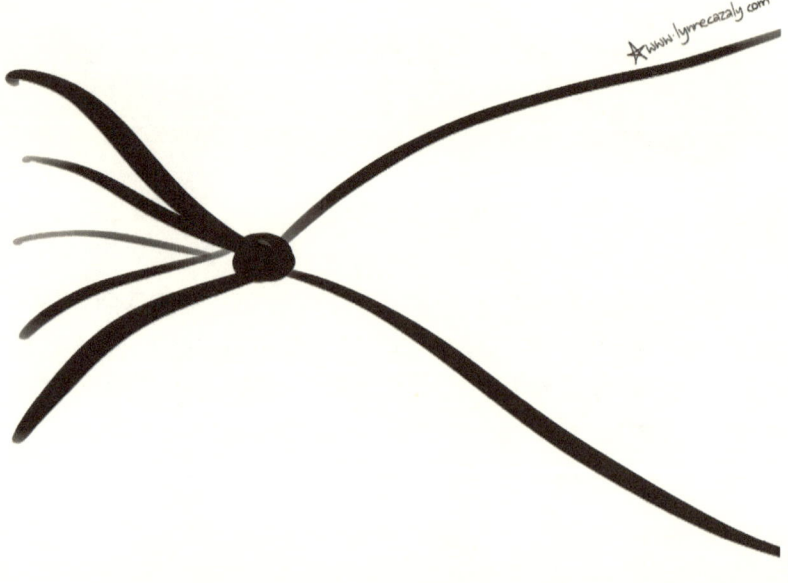

If you sync and then allow people to work independently and asynchronously and then reconnect sync, at a time in the future, then you are likely to be working better with sync async.

I believe there needs to be a kind of pattern or rhythm – and it doesn't need to be an equal rhythm – to allow for both synchronous and asynchronous work.

In the main, I would be going for more asynchronous work and minimize synchronous meetings, so they are held only to deliver or create high value and high impact.

Over the course of a project or piece of work it could look like this:

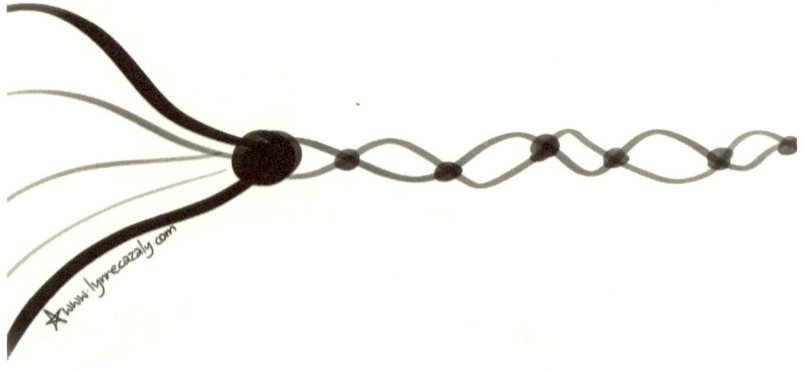

→ If you were to visualize what your sync async pattern looks like for the work you're doing on a project or piece of work, do you:

- come together sync and then never again?
- do you never come together sync?
- do you come together and stay together sync?
- do you come together and apart over time in a sync async kind of rhythm or pattern?

Where else could you async?

Beyond work or learning, where else could you use synchronous and asynchronous work?

A friend mentioned the value in having the parent teacher conversation and meeting at her child's school go remote and online. Instead of driving to the school, parking, waiting around, and a range of other things that don't only take time but take effort, energy, fuel and resources, the online version was easier.

In a way, report cards are an asynchronous form of communication. Could they become even more async by having some more back-and-forth such as, you answer the questions based on how you think your child has gone, and your child does too, and the teacher will too, and then 'let's have a sync conversation about it.

Where else could asynchronous work be used?

Building a property?

Planning a holiday? My husband Michael and I do this kind of planning. He starts a spreadsheet with a few dates and locations (and the kilometres to drive or the estimated cost). I review it and add in my notes about where else I'd like to go. Then we go out for drinks or dinner and sync on it. We discover, explore and decide. Then he goes off and books the accommodation and camping sites and I go off and make lists for meals, packing and must-do things prior to departure.

Using a tour guide? When you hire one of those audio description guides in a museum or other tourist attraction, you're leveraging async. It's not being read to you live. It was pre-recorded by someone in a recording studio. Genius!

→ *How could you be a tour guide for a project, piece of work or initiative? Could you create a series of audio descriptions just like a museum does?*

Learning to cook? Hey, any YouTube video is basically async. It was recorded previously and you're there, watching it, looking, following the steps, listening, pausing, rewinding, watching that bit again - what did they say? Sear for how long? - and then you carry on.

→: *How could you create a 'cooking' experience to deliver insights, learning or training in a more async way?*

Getting your medical test results?

Working with a life coach?

Doing an assessment?

Learning a skill?

Negotiating a contract?

Confirming a proposal?

Revising a quotation?

Sync async doesn't only belong in our work or during working hours. It can free up time and pressure and help us live in ways that are more about our choice and preferences.

Next Steps

Keep building skill

As you try some more sync async skills, tools and techniques, remember to keep building skill that will benefit better sync situations and more effective async work.

Here are some suggestions:

REDUCE these behaviours and skills	BUILD these behaviours and skills
Over-explaining	Improvisation
Waffling	Facilitation
Assuming	Iteration
Hoarding information	Framing
Holding up information	Questioning
Holding on to information	Clarifying
Withholding information	Checking and checklists
Holding court	Confirming
Speaking without structure	Note taking
Talking over others	Working out loud
Monopolising meeting time	Glossary of terms
Interrupting	Summarising
I me my-ing /all about me	Sensemaking
Perfectionism	Synopsis-ising

Improvise and experiment

This is kind of a big improvisation. It doesn't mean you don't know what's going to happen or don't have any control. You have. You can have greater control over which things are done sync and which are done async. You can ask the team or your colleagues. You can start sync. Or I'd love that you started async.

Incrementally asynchronous

Not one single way of working sync async is going to work for everyone. This is part of the evolution and growth of it in your team, group or organisation. You can start using one or two of the sync async skills, tools and techniques before you start doing it with greater global intent. A start is a start. And then you can improve or grow more async, bit by bit, incrementally, over time.

You can read more about increments and iterations in my book 'ish: The Problem with our Pursuit for Perfection and the Life-Changing Practice of Good Enough'.

Lynne Cazaly

Summary

When we give up our time to join others in synchronous situations, we're making decisions and choices that can make us less effective than we could be.

There are easier ways to work – which you're already using; so, start using them more often.

Ask yourself questions like:

- Could I have done this async?
- Could this be better for others if it were async?
- Might this suit more people and involve more people if it was async?
- Why do we absolutely need to make this sync?'

We already work on things alone and together with others. We don't need to default to everyone, all the time … or even most of the time.

We can stop involving everybody or large groups of people in everything in real time. We still want to involve people, but we can include people and consider people, in ways that leverage many more choices, options, tech and tools.

From research on companies who reduced meetings, to the motivating benefits of small wins, working asynchronously is one of the clear changes we can make every single day of the week when the 'ding' of an invitation arrives in our schedule or inbox.

Try more asynchronous work. And don't wait for your leader, team, or organization to do this. You can start doing it, now.

Try it today. Look at a meeting that you have scheduled or have been invited to in your diary, and don't attend it. Instead collect your thoughts on the topics and the agenda items and send them through to the meeting leader or convener prior to the meeting.

Send your apologies and say that you have already collected your thoughts. Include a note that if they want even more input from you or need to consult with you further, that you would love to provide them with more input.

After the meeting, check in with others who were there and get a summary about what happened.

We don't just cancel; we can clarify and specify with our questions of others about why being there is vital.

And we gain a reduction in stress and overwhelm, and an increase in engagement, trust and our feelings of value.

We can get ourselves that precious clear air, quiet time, gaps and blocks where we're able to do the more important work or the deeper, more complex thinking and creating.

This is not anti-collaboration; it is pro-progress.

Sync async is a way of working, not just a way of communicating. Think broader than communication.

Async work at its simplest allows us to work with fewer interruptions. We can be more efficient and take better care of ourselves and our colleagues.

Importantly, it uses less energy, resources, people and things. That means there's less wastage which is better for the world we live in.

Async has been shown to deliver value sooner - even if the task or project isn't fully completed - it's often in a state where feedback and input is greater, tweaks are more meaningful and valuable and the path to completion is smoother because more progress has already been made.

Rather than rushing, racing and stressing through important work, working sync async gives us scope to spend more time on the important stuff. We can allocate thinking, energy, time and resources to where it's truly required.

And when we do sync in person, let's make them valuable, impactful and memorable experiences, worthy of our involvement and contribution.

To make progress easier, take the next best step.

What could I do on this next? Sending a meeting request is potentially not the right answer.

Try something async instead.

Lynne Cazaly

There are those who value your labour and not your life.

They will be offended by your boundaries.

Set them anyway.

You are worthy of care.

- Dr Thema Bryant

References

Amabile, Teresa M and Kramer, Steven J. 'The Power of Small Wins'. Harvard Business Review. May 2011. https://hbr.org/2011/05/the-power-of-small-wins

Blair, Elizabeth. Virtual 'Love Sweet Love' From Quarantined Berklee College of Music Students. NPR. 24 Mar 2020 https://www.npr.org/sections/coronavirus-live-updates/2020/03/24/821041006/virtual-love-sweet-love-from-quarantined-berklee-college-of-music-students

Burgess, Maree. *Level Up How Leaders Do Less and Be More.* Grammar Factory Publishing, 2021.

Cross, Rob, et al. "Collaboration Overload Is Sinking Productivity." *Harvard Business Review*, Harvard Business School Publishing, 7 Sept. 2021, https://hbr.org/2021/09/collaboration-overload-is-sinking-productivity

Duncan, Rodger Dean. "Is Your Collaboration Overused and Underwhelming? Here's A Fix." *Forbes*, Forbes Magazine, 7 Dec. 2021, https://www.forbes.com/sites/rodgerdeanduncan/2021/12/07/is-your-collaboration-overused-and-underwhelming-heres-a-fix

Fong, Kenzo. "The Future of Work Is Asynchronous." *Fast Company*, Mansueto Ventures, LLC, 18 Jan. 2022, https://www.fastcompany.com/90712513/the-future-of-work-is-asynchronous

Fox, Jason. *How to Lead A Quest: A Handbook for Pioneering Executives.* John Wiley and Sons Australia, Ltd, 2016.

Glaveski, Steve. "Remote Work Should Be (Mostly) Asynchronous." *Harvard Business Review*, Harvard Business School Publishing, 1 Dec. 2021, https://hbr.org/2021/12/remote-work-should-be-mostly-asynchronous

Gourani, Soulaima. 'Why Most Meetings Fail Before They Even Begin'. Forbes. 6 May 2021

Grogono, Jen. "CEOs: How To Start An Employee-Facing Podcast". Forbes. 16 Sept 2020. https://www.forbes.com/sites/forbestechcouncil/2020/09/16/ceos-how-to-start-an-employee-facing-podcast

Jacobson, Greg. "Real Life Examples of the 7 Wastes of Lean (Plus 1)." *KaiNexus*, 12 Apr. 2021, https://blog.kainexus.com/improvement-disciplines/lean/7-wastes-of-lean/real-life-examples.

Laker, Ben; Vijay Pereira, Vijay; Budhwar, Pawan; and Malik, Ashish. 'The surprising impact of meeting free days'. MIT Sloan Management Review. 18 Jan. 2022. https://sloanreview.mit.edu/article/the-surprising-impact-of-meeting-free-days/

Laker, Ben, et al. "Dear Manager, You're Holding Too Many Meetings." *Harvard Business Review*, Harvard Business School Publishing, 9 Mar. 2022, https://hbr.org/2022/03/dear-manager-youre-holding-too-many-meetings.

Laker, Ben, et al. "Impact of Fewer Meetings." *Harvard Business Review*, Harvard Business School Publishing, 24 Mar. 2022, https://hbr.org/data-visuals/2022/03/impact-of-fewer-meetings.

Lebre, Marcelo. "Why You Should Be Working Asynchronously in 2022." *Remote*, Remote Technology, Inc., https://remote.com/blog/why-you-should-be-doing-async-work.

Linda Stone, https://lindastone.net/.

Perlow, Leslie A; Hadley, Constance Noonan and Eun, Eunice. 'Stop the Meeting Madness'. Harvard Business Review. July August 2017.

Romm, Cari. "Psychologists Explain Your Phone Anxiety (and How to Get over It)." *The Cut*, Vox Media, LLC., 13 Aug. 2020, https://www.thecut.com/article/psychologists-explain-your-phone-anxiety.html.

Spataro, Jared. "5 Key Trends Leaders Need to Understand to Get Hybrid Right." *Harvard Business Review*, Harvard Business School Publishing, 16 Mar. 2022, https://hbr.org/2022/03/5-key-trends-leaders-need-to-understand-to-get-hybrid-right

Stanier, James, et al. "What Great Hybrid Cultures Do Differently." *Harvard Business Review*, Harvard Business School Publishing, 16 Mar. 2022, https://hbr.org/2022/03/what-great-hybrid-cultures-do-differently

Steel, Julia. 'Unite'. 2020

Taylor, Chris. 'Subtitles are the future. Sorry, caption haters.' Mashable. 28 October 2021. https://mashable.com/article/subtitles-captions-tv-movies-streaming

Warner, Jeremy. "China's Fresh Covid Nightmare Is a Painful Reminder." *The Sydney Morning Herald*, The Sydney Morning Herald, 8 Apr. 2022, https://www.smh.com.au/business/the-economy/china-s-fresh-covid-nightmare-is-a-painful-reminder-20220408-p5abvr.html.

"Too Much Togetherness? the Downside of Workplace Collaboration." *Knowledge at Wharton*, Knowledge at Wharton, 9 Nov. 2017, http://knowledge.wharton.upenn.edu/article/much-togetherness-downside-workplace-collaboration/.

About the Author

Lynne Cazaly CSP

Lynne Cazaly helps individuals, teams and businesses transition to new and creative ways of thinking and working.

She is an international keynote speaker and a Certified Speaking Professional, a designation awarded by the Professional Speakers Association. She is a multi-award-winning author and a master facilitator.

Lynne Cazaly is the author of 10 books and a contributing author to 3 more.

She is an experienced radio broadcaster, presenter and

producer having presented more than 10000 hours on-air. Her background is as a communication specialist, having lectured in under-graduate and post-graduate programs in several of Australia's Universities and consulting to different industries and sectors on communication, change and transformation.

Lynne can help you think better, make sense of information and handle the realities of the modern workplace by tackling overwhelm, workload and information overload, with her clever hacks and creative and ingenious processes, tools and methods.

She is an experienced board director and chair and an #avgeek, loving everything aviation, helicopters and air traffic control. She enjoys remote area travel across the Australian outback with her husband Michael and lives in Melbourne, Australia.

For Australian Rules Football/AFL football fans, she is a descendent of Roy 'Up There' Cazaly, about whom the song 'Up There Cazaly' was written.

See more at www.lynnecazaly.com

For keynote speaking, workshops and facilitated sessions, contact Lynne Cazaly at info@lynnecazaly.com

We can sync async it all!

⭐ www.lynnecazaly.com

Lynne Cazaly

Also by the Author

www.lynnecazaly.com

- Argh! Too Much Information, Not Enough Brain: A Practical Guide to Outsmarting Overwhelm
- Better Ways of Thinking and Working: How Changing the Way You Do Things, Changes What You Can Do
- ish: The Problem with our Pursuit for Perfection and the Life-Changing Practice of Good Enough
- Agile-ish: How to Create a Culture of Agility
- Ideas Book: A Journal of Templates and Tools for Thinking
- Leader as Facilitator: How to Engage, Inspire and Get Work Done
- Making Sense: A Handbook for the Future of Work
- Create Change: How to Apply Innovation in an Era of Uncertainty
- Visual Mojo: How to Capture Thinking, Convey Information and Collaborate Using Visuals.

And a contributing author to:
- Unite
- What the hell do we do now: An enterprise guide to COVID-19 and beyond
- The World of Visual Facilitation: Unlock your Power to Connect People & Ideas

Making progress easier
in the changing world of work

LYNNE CAZALY

www.ingramcontent.com/pod-product-compliance
Lightning Source LLC
Chambersburg PA
CBHW020321010526
44107CB00054B/1928